Ancestral Lines Clearing

Ancestral Lines Clearing

Mary Phyllis Horn

M.Ed., Shaman, Certified Therapist
Interfaith Metaphysical Minister

Ancestral Lines Clearing is one of numerous modalities contained in previous compilations:
Finishing Up All Lives On The Planet, First Edition copyright 1999, Second Edition copyright 2000. Living Light Publisher. ISBN 0-9709168-0-9
Healing This Life, A Shamanic Path To Freedom And Wholeness, copyright 2002, Living Light Publisher. ISBN 0-9709168-2-5

Library of Congress Cataloguing-in-Publication Data
Horn, Mary Phyllis 1939-
     Ancestral Lines Clearing / Mary Phyllis Horn
     Includes bibliographical references
     ISBN 978-1482049473
     1. Shamanism.   2. Ancestral Lines   3. Metaphysics
     4. New Age   5. Hypnotherapy   6. Spiritual
     7. Spiritual Healing   8. Huna   9. Title

The Center of the Living Light
24 Creekside Circle, Pittsboro, NC 27312

Printed in the U.S.A. by CreateSpace Publishers

Dedication

to Spirit,

and to all of you who accept

the healing Spirit left on your "doorstep."

Acknowledgements

Much gratitude goes to all of my clients and students who consented to have the stories of their Ancestral Lines Clearing© reported in this book. Their beautiful work brings clarity to the use of the various healing methods divulged here. The names printed with their reports are aliases, in order to protect their anonymity.

Thank you to Barbs Burman for her editing comments and inspirational support to the very spirit of the message and writings within this book.

A special note of thanks goes to the late Reverends Stan and Helen Ainsworth for their gift of the Forgiveness Method script which they adapted from the Hawaiian Huna "Ho'oponopono" rite. In turn, I have expanded upon it to suit the needs of Ancestral Lines Clearing.

Most of all, deepest gratitude goes to Spirit, i.e., Divine Source, my High Self, Spirit Teacher and Spirit Helpers, for their faithful support, encouragement, and persistent insistence that I write this book.

Table of Contents

Introduction   i
    DNA Patterns
    The Nature of Time
    Ability to Get Prayer Results

Chapters

  One: The Original Channeling   1
    Huna Basis
    "Doorstep" Offering

  Two: Benefits of Ancestral Lines Clearing   7
    Initial Outcomes
    Client and Student Reports

  Three: Huna   15
    Hawaiian Shamanism
    The Triune Self
    Developing Inner Rapport and Focus
    Client's Experience
    Meditation, Prayer, Spiritual Cleansing

  Four: Ho'oponopono aka Forgiveness   29
    What "Forgiveness" Is
    Client's Experience
    Why and How Forgiveness Works
    Ho'oponopono Scripts

  Five: High Energies Needed   37
    Aura Cleansing and the Archangels
    High Powered Spiritual Energies
    Mind-Set for Working with Spirit

Six: Preparation for the Work   **45**
Aspect of Your Healing Issue To Use
Modalities for Clearing
Components of the Clearing Process
Client's Experience

Seven: Full Walk Through   **51**
Modalities Preparation
Ho'oponopono Within the Clearing
Working with the High Self
Clearing Your Future

Eight: Variations in the Process   **59**
Configurations and Other Variations
Energy Healing
Ancestral Lines Healing
Client and Student Experiences

Nine: Personal Follow-ups   **67**
Others' Soul Part Removals
Changing Beliefs
Client and Student Experiences

Ten: Ancestral Lines Clearing Scripts   **77**
Clearing Each Side of Your Family
Clearing Your Future
"Doorstep" Offering
Personal Follow-ups
Anchoring the Healing

Eleven: My Shamanic Path   **81**
Shamanic Signposts
Reluctant Shaman
Surrendering to the Path
My Educational Background

Glossary   **v**
Metaphysical Terms
Psychological Terms
Shamanic Terms
Spiritual Terms

Bibliography   **xi**

Resources   **xiii**

Introduction

In the DNA of ancestral lines there are beautiful traits as well as undesirable ones. The two can become intertwined. Negative traits can distort, corrupt, contaminate or completely hide the positive. Yet the positive is still latent within you and your ancestral lines. Unfortunately, the negativity can keep you from expressing your beauties in a pure way, or in a way that otherwise would help and inspire others. It can even cause others to reject your beauties no matter how well you express them.

The methods Spirit channeled to me clear away the negative, dysfunctional, limiting traits of your ancestral lines no matter how many generations back in time they started. Once the negative traits are removed, the family beauties become free to blossom fully as intended. An analogy to this would be like removing barnacles from a ship so that the vessel can sail easily, smoothly and beautifully as it was designed to do.

There is an old adage that says, "We cannot change what happened, but we can change our attitude toward it." In so doing, we change our lives and our future experiences. This is usually viewed as "the only thing we can change about the past is our attitude towards it." Yet people have reported miraculous healing from doing a past-life regression to the cause of a persistent pain that medicine cannot resolve. It is generally assumed that the person experiencing the regression is still working on mere memory and attitude alone.

In the Ancestral Lines Clearing process there are instances in which Spirit will direct you to forgive the ancient past even though no details are revealed that could give you a reason why. And even if they did arise why would forgiveness, now, affect and remove blocks to the past? In this book are numerous reports of family members making miraculous changes despite knowing nothing about Ancestral Lines Clearing©, much less that one of their family was engaged in a special metaphysical healing modality.

What I am saying is that Ancestral Lines Clearing does more than just change your attitude. It actually changes circumstances in the past in a way that also changes current relatives in your ancestry. That is, if they accept Spirit's offering of the change. It is an individual decision, as it should be, with free will.

The Nature of Time

This discussion gets us to the subject of the nature of time. In a way, there is a misconception about it: that time moves ever forward, not backward except for accessing memories. In shamanic journeying it is commonly known that the dimensions journeyed to are outside of time and space; in that sense, all of time is occurring simultaneously. There is what is called "past" and "future," but both can be experienced in the "now" of any given moment. In that sense, past, present and future are all one, all in the "now." In shamanic journeying we can easily access the very distant past, whether of our own life history or for someone else; the same is true of the future. Past events can be changed if Spirit gives permission. Future events can be changed largely by human will and are constantly in a state of flux. Current decisions change the future and every human is constantly making decisions. That is why the future is so nebulous and unpredictable; we do not know from moment to moment what other people are going to decide.

To my clairvoyant perception, the path of time looks like a path found in the physical world. It can be traversed forward and back in space as well as time. Within the context of this "simultaneous time" it is noticeable that personal attitude and forgiveness can affect the past, every bit as much as it affects the present and the future. Time travel to the past, with mind and spirit, is not done merely by human volition. Rather, it is done under the authorization and auspices of Spirit. In Ancestral Lines Clearing it is actually Spirit who does the travel. We humans are involved as well, as a partner to Spirit.

We are required to witness what Spirit is doing, and to do the forgiveness ritual when there is a block.

DNA Pattern in Your Ancestral Lines

When faced with a recurring issue, you are at a decision point for the future. Are you going to bring the past into the future as a mere recapitulation? Or will you forgive the painful past, release it, and choose a different future? That different future will stay different from the past if it is not interfered with by your ancestral lines. Where a pattern has been cemented into your DNA, it acts like a subliminal suggestion. It moves you into the old pattern without your realizing it. All of a sudden you witness, to your dismay, the reoccurance of an old pattern you thought you had healed.

Now, think of yourself at the head of a conjunction of many streams, those streams being the patterns set into your DNA by your ancestry. The pattern continues to be reinforced into your DNA by every living family member now. They may know nothing of Ancestral Lines Clearing. But you do. You have been led to this book and possible acceptance of this awareness. That says, to me at least, that Spirit is giving you authorization to make a beneficial change not only for yourself but also for all of your family members, living or dead. Spirit is giving you the choice: do you want to be the spearhead of all your ancestral lines coming through you to the future? That is, are you ready to be the spokesperson for them? All it takes is recognition within yourself that there is a pattern you dislike, that it is also found in other family members whether you realize it or not, and that you want it gone from you! Spirit will change it for you. Then, through your permission (free will), Spirit will offer it to all other living family members, known and unknown, to take the healing as they choose. I stress "offer" because Spirit will not violate any human's free will.

Based on Hawaiian "Ho'oponopono"

Ancestral Lines Clearing is based on the Huna "Ho'oponopono" ritual of forgiveness. However, forgiveness alone does not change what is already written into your family's DNA. Spirit has to be intimately involved in the process, to clear the DNA. Spirit wielding a very high-powered form of energy creates a much deeper release of negative energy. Ancestral Lines Clearing© uses the forgiveness rite because we humans are involved; the release goes deeper with Ancestral Lines Clearing because Spirit's very high-powered energy is actively involved. That process is delineated in this book.

If you are able to call in Spirit and maintain continuity of focus on what Spirit does, you are telling it that you are ready to let it continue its work on your behalf. Ability to call in Spirit and actually see what it does for you is what I call "getting results from prayer." This ability is crucial for doing your own Ancestral Lines Clearing. It is crucial for calling in your own High Self, the Archangels, or high-powered healing guides. It is crucial for maintaining awareness of Spirit's presence, for staying aware of what it is doing during the clearing, for knowing when there is a block and when the healing is finished.

There are layers involved here and we each have our own part in it. If you cannot yet call in Spirit well enough to do an Ancestral Lines Clearing for yourself, all is not lost. You can enlist an energy worker to do it for you. The chapter on "Preparation For The Work" will advise you of what to look for in such a person. Understand, however, that even though you enlist the help of an energy worker you still have a crucial role to play in obtaining results: staying receptive to what is happening and sincerely wanting the truth no matter how it shows up.

Service to the World

Think of the tens of thousands even millions of people genetically connected to you from the time of your family origins up to the present! Each time you do this work, you lessen the burden of spiritual growth for yourself and for all of those other people in your ancestry, known to you or not. In essence, by clearing your family lines of a dysfunction, you are significantly helping willing members of the entire human race to heal, even though they may not know how the change came about.

I am writing this book so that you too can start on the path of healing yourself and your ancestral lines. Each chapter describes important components of the process, much in the order it was initially given to me. Personal, client and student stories serve as illustrations of parts of the process.

Chapter One

The Original Channeling

I first heard of "Ancestral Lines Clearing" from my upper world Spirit Teacher in 1996 after a pleasant visit with my father in Pennsylvania. About two weeks after that visit I was quite puzzled to feel one of his undesirable attitudes spring up within me. So I did a journey to the upper world and asked my Spirit Teacher "what's going on?! I thought I had healed this!" He said, "You did. This attitude isn't from you and it's also not from your father. It's from the Horn family lines." Well, at first I did not believe that. Then he brought to 1 my mind the faces of one aunt and two uncles, each showing a similar but less pronounced attitude on their faces than Dad's. I understood what my Spirit Teacher was conveying, and asked him to help me clear it. He said, "We can do that, but it will only return over and over the rest of your life; you'll be repeatedly sabotaged unless you clear your family's ancestral lines."

He went on to explain, as a metaphorical illustration. "If your parents were alcoholics then you would know clearly where your dysfunctional attitudes and behaviors were coming from and you could easily release them. If your grandparents were alcoholics then you could likewise discover where your dysfunctional attitudes and behaviors were coming from and change them. But if the alcoholism occurred more generations ago than that and no recent generations carry it, it is extremely difficult to uncover the true cause of the dysfunctions you have. This is especially so if there are no family stories about preceding generations. The farther back in time an issue originated, the more insidious and pervasive it is within the ancestral lines. The dysfunctional behaviors and attitudes become ingrained in the family even to the point of entering your physical DNA."

"OK...So how do I do the clearing?" I asked.

Energy Healing From Spirit

My Spirit Teacher proceeded to show me a rather extensive yet simple set of patterns that are done energetically, not intellectually. The patterns remove the energy (spiritual vibration) of a detrimental thread of DNA directly related to the person's ancestral line "issue" so that the ancestral lines can thrive on the positives instead of being locked into a dysfunctional pattern. The detriment shows up as a distortion in the vibrations, rather than a story that the vibration causes in our human way of thinking and feeling. He went on to say, "Just knowing your family's genealogy will not remove the detrimental DNA. In fact, people can be adopted, not know who their parents are, and still be able to clear their family lines productively. This is because Spirit alone knows where the detrimental energy is and has the higher spiritual authorization and power to remove it."

The form of Ancestral Lines Clearing he taught me is done energetically and under the auspices of highest Spirit. It usually does not reveal insights or details of preceding generations except where there are pivotal points in the development of the dysfunction. Spirit tells us only as much as is needed to release the trait. Pivotal points may be the actual onset of the dysfunction or they may not be. In some instances the onset may be minuscule and would eventually have dissipated had it not been for a trauma at a later time period. At the occurrence of that trauma, the dysfunction locked into the ancestral lines.

Huna Basis

The pattern my Spirit Teacher taught me is based on Huna principles which I had studied fifteen years before. These principles have proved to be of profound benefit to my inner life. Huna is the name Max Freedom Long gave to the spiritual lore he discovered embedded in the Hawaiian language. The first Huna component my Spirit Teacher addressed was the "Ho'oponopono," ie., a tribal forgiveness ritual. The Hawaiian shamans, i.e., Kahunas, performed that ritual in the physical presence of anyone in their tribe who needed it. I find the process to be just as effective within our minds as in person because Spirit can be proxy for all individuals involved. The high spiritual being who did the clearing of the lines for me is my own High Self. The "High Self" is the Huna term for the highest Mother-Father God we can envision who watches over us, gives guidance, answers prayer, governs karma and has jurisdiction over our spirit helpers.

In the first step of the Ancestral Lines Clearing, my Spirit Teacher directed me to do the Ho'oponopono for everyone I ever knew or had heard about, living or dead, on my father's side of the family; this included preceding generations as well as present and future generations already living. I did the forgiveness ritual with them in group format until everyone spontaneously vanished from that inner scene that I was envisioning. I knew instinctively that their spirit had given and accepted the forgiveness.

High Self Clears the Lines

After that, as part of the second step, my High Self came into view. Using a powerful laser-like beam of light that also exuded a faint crackling sound like an electrical buzz, he cleared the family lines of the dysfunctional trait addressed. My Spirit Teacher required me to watch what transpired; other than that, I did none of the clearing work. At one point, the beam dwindled down to nothing and revealed a scene several hundred years earlier than now; instinctively I knew the clearing was not yet finished. My Spirit Teacher had me perform the Ho'oponopono rite to that time period even though I had no clue of what had transpired. It felt right to let that happen, and the energy picked up again once the ritual was completed. I noticed that all of this laser-like clearing was following a path directly south, skirting the western limits of where I usually do past-life work. No sooner did I realize that, then the path made a sharp turn to the left. The clearing proceeded due east, now skirting the southern-most limits of the past-life field. This time when the white light stopped, I knew the work was finished. Although an image of a group of people emerged, no illustration of the cause of Dad's attitude came up.

My Spirit Teacher told me to ask my High Self to replenish my energy. Instantly I felt rejuvenated. Then he said we were to do the same process with my mother's family lines as we did my Dad's, and on the very same issue. "Why?!" I exclaimed, "she didn't evidence that personality quirk!" "True," he replied, "but she abetted it. She didn't do anything to stop your father from using it." So then I commenced with the same forgiveness ritual and clearing of Mom's family lines that I had done with Dad's. The work followed the same southern and eastern path as Dad's did. It also went much more swiftly.

The Future

The final clearing stage was to direct my High Self to clear my own life's future, up through and beyond my death. Again I questioned my Spirit Teacher's rationale for this. He said, "It is Spirit's will that no human be tempted nor pushed beyond capacity to endure. This is a planet for learning and spiritual growth, not one for self-destruction. If taking on a current volley of ancestral lines negativity would otherwise cause your soul to self-destruct, We (Spirit) divert that negative energy to a point in the future where you can more easily and safely deal with it. That is one of the causes for the negative pattern recycling in your life."

This time, I did not have to say the Ho'oponopono rite at the beginning of the clearing. Instead, it was used only if there was a block somewhere in the future. When this was done, he had me ask my High Self to replenish my energy.

"Doorstep" Offering

The last part of the Ancestral Lines Clearing process is for the High Self to energetically bring the healing up to the "doorstep" of all living family members. My Spirit Teacher said this had to be done in order for the trait to be removed from the family lines. Even though these people usually have no clue of the work we are doing, Spirit authorizes the energetic action and allows each person's High Self to give it to family members at the right time in their lives. (There have even been a few instances in which someone's High Self did not allow Spirit to bring the healing to the doorstep of a specific member of the family because that member would accept it...and it would have led to their downfall.) In all cases, Spirit is in charge.

My Spirit Teacher stressed the word "doorstep" because the healing could not be taken directly into family members without interfering with their free will; they have to give their permission. "Doorstep" allows them to reach out and take the healing or to leave it. We humans have free will. We also each have our own spiritual life work to accomplish and we may not be ready for this gift of healing. Let us say, in a hypothetical example, that Joe Blow does Ancestral Lines Clearing on a family trait of aggressiveness. He may need to do that because he is overly aggressive with other people. But what about his timid sister Suzie Blow? She may need that aggressive trait in order to summon up the courage to leave the house everyday for her job. If Joe were to take the healing into her life, she would not have even that amount of energy, and would find herself house-bound, without a job. In other words, it would do her great disservice, while also infringing upon her free will. For her, aggressiveness is a necessary virtue; for him, it is a downfall. When we take our healing up to the doorstep of living family members, we leave it there, respecting their prerogative to embrace it or not. The ones who innately accept the healing, exhibit positive changes.

The last part of the Ancestral Lines Clearing is to take the healing to the "doorstep" of all living members of the family regardless of which generation their family was linked into ours. Think of the spider-web-effect of all the interlinking of families throughout all generations of one family! There may be thousands or millions of people in the world who would be beneficially affected by just one person's clearing. Spirit locates and determines who is to be offered the healing.

At the end of my fifteen-minute session of Ancestral Lines Clearing, I felt a whoosh of clarity equivalent to lifting twenty-five pounds of weight off me. The air felt cooler and clearer.

Dad's uncomfortable attitude has not reoccured.

Chapter Two

Benefits of Ancestral Lines Clearing

How can Ancestral Lines Clearing possibly be so effective, and why is it so important to our planet? Scientists are now saying that indeed the DNA is changeable, in fact, a lot more than originally thought. People have been saying that also about Ancestral Lines Clearing ever since 1996. Spirit is actively at work here, to help anyone who is willing to make the requisite changes.

In various workshops and private sessions people experienced beneficial changes immediately. Some said it felt like a gentle wind going through every molecule of their body, clearing away unwanted material. A friend said she could feel a "wind blowing through my pores and cells." Many have said, "It feels like my DNA has been changed!" Several could feel the energy traversing their spine or working with their chakras. Others reported feeling heavy energy releasing, resulting in freedom, lightness, and more joy. Many report that after they did this work, their family members, who did not know anything about the process, exhibited positive changes and became more congenial.

In a private session one client completely cleared a complex issue within ten minutes. Witnessing my amazement at that, she divulged that her sister had been to see me several years before and had told her only that she had spent over an hour doing some kind of ancestral work. I grinned and said,

"Then thank your sister for your quick progress! She brought it up to your doorstep."

My personal story: *I taught a workshop on Ancestral Lines Clearing in Raleigh, NC. When the class was in the process of bringing the healing up to the doorstep of every living family member, I suddenly felt a "whoosh" of clarity and well-being come into me from the direction of a blonde-haired woman. After the class shared their experiences, I told her what I had felt. I also asked her if her ancestry were Norwegian (as is my mother's). She smiled softly and nodded her head. I thanked her for the healing.*

Others' Experiences

To give you a more graphic idea of the benefits of this work, I include below numerous reports from students and clients, using alias names to assure their anonymity. These reports include benefits in their own lives, in those of their family and sometimes in the world, after doing an Ancestral Lines Clearing.

"Gina" took my workshop in Ancestral Lines Clearing. *She had suffered persistent physical abuse as a child, and spent much of her adult years in various forms of therapy to recover from it. When she came to my workshop, she expected to deal with the abuse pattern as a whole. However, her High Self told her to focus only on the "attitude" involved in abuse. Disappointed, yet respectful of Spirit, she agreed. When she and all of the other workshop participants finished clearing the first side of their families, tears were streaming down her face. She said that the healing she had just experienced with her father's lineage was huge. When everyone finished clearing the other side of the family, her whole demeanor was much different; she was noticeably calm and relaxed. She said the clearing brought her a sense of relief.*

About ten days later, she called me on the phone to tell of her experiences since the workshop. She had attained even deeper healing personally, and was extremely grateful for that. But that was not the reason she called. Her voice was shaky; it was all she could do to hold back tears. She said a distant cousin of hers, "a very distant cousin," was a *workaholic and abuser of his wife and children. He was, in her words, "a <u>not nice man</u>." In the ten days since the workshop, of which he had no knowledge, he was no longer a workaholic. He was a kindly gentle grandfather, no longer abusing his family. (Wow!) Gina knew this change was the result of the work we had done.*

We both agreed that the sudden and profound change in him was a testament to the Ancestral Lines Clearing format that Spirit channeled. I also affirmed to her that it was a testament to her ability to call in her High Self to wield the necessary high-powered clearing energy...and further, that her cousin obviously had been praying for help. In all probability he had become a workaholic in order to avoid abusing his wife and children. Meaning, he could not help himself. He stayed away from home as long as he could, because he knew that the moment he stepped inside the house he would not be able to keep himself from abusing his beloved family. The immediacy of his change told me that he must have been praying desperately for spiritual aid. He got it, through Gina's and Spirit's work.

"Gene" did an Ancestral Lines Clearing on lack of abundance. On one side of his family he and many relatives were public school teachers. This is a profession notorious for its low pay; he could not support his family on his salary alone. His wife had to work a full time job in order to help out. On the other side of his family many of the men either exhibited an attitude of entitlement or otherwise chose work that was low paying. I do not recall what aspect of abundance he chose, but whatever it was, the clearing healed both him and close members of his family.

In the workshop, the time came for bringing the healing up to the "doorstep of living family members." In the inner visualization given to him by Spirit, he "saw" his sister and cousin step in to take the healing even before he had finished the request to his High Self. Both women were used to a comfortable income, obviously abundant to begin with. One of his brothers tentatively took a portion of the healing. He had been doing alright but had to be frugal about his expenses. The other brother backed into the shadows silently saying, "not me." At the time, he had gone through bankruptcy of his business and was contemplating personal bankruptcy.

Several months later the latter brother called Gene to tell him that he was doing very well now, and was going on vacation to Europe. Within a year of that, he bought a condo in the French Alps and another in the Bahamas. Gene's other brother had received a promotion with a good pay hike. His sister and aunt were now making well into the six-figure income range. Gene himself had accepted a university teaching job that gave him an income significantly higher than any year of his public school teaching.

It is interesting how each family member may accept the healing in a way and time of their own choosing.

"Maya's" personal issue was to clear her ancestral lines of fear. *She thought she would be addressing only one of her fears. However, her High Self said to address "fear itself" and then all the details would be healed as well: Fear of letting go of the familiar; fear of failing, exploring, practicing a new way of making a living, taking a new direction, a new path, fully walking a new path, committing to a new way of income, letting go of what is no longer working, losing the status of "making it" by starting a new venture, changing, transitioning from cubicle desk to free-range career to entrepreneurship, transitioning to more freedom; and fear of not being able to care for her family if she lives as an artist.*

About a month after the workshop, she said that nearly all of the fears had gone, resulting in positive changes in her life. Regarding letting go of the familiar and fear of failing, this was still in process. She had not yet left her full time job. In preparation for doing so, she was in the process of setting up office hours in a local center, working with a brand for her business, and working with a consultant for business details. She also was making strides towards transition from cubicle to free-range career to entrepreneurship.

On the other hand, in many other areas where she had previously felt fear, the healing has held. She said she also had put away her tangible achievements, such as trophies, in her previous career and had excitedly found that other people were not treating her any differently. Such a relief!

At the time Maya sent me this report, she still feared not being able to take care of her family if she were to live as an artist. She surmised that she still needed to sit down and figure out exactly how much she needed to make, for this to happen.

A year after the workshop she resigned her full-time job. Her artistic endeavor is now 'taking off big time' with requests for her work coming in from all directions around the country and the world. Her comment to me was: "I am so glad that my spirit teacher instructed me to tackle fear. Without that being taken care of I could not do all the things I am doing right now."

Maya continued: "Part of my artistic entrepreneurship is channeling information from my family lines. Recently my seven year old son did the same thing. He listened to me composing a melody on my new guitar. Within a day or so, he picked up that same guitar and played the melody he had heard me play. The significance of it was that he played it a couple octaves higher than I had! I could play only on the lower frets of the guitar, so there is no way he could have seen me play that high! It is obvious that he accepted the 'doorstep' healing and was now channeling our ancestral lines too."

"Rosalee" received a soul retrieval of a soul part that left when she was still in her mother's womb. It had left her vulnerable to her family's genetic predisposition toward moroseness, i.e., a habit of depression. When it returned, she felt resistant to even talk with her soul part. Her spirit guides advised doing an Ancestral Lines Clearing, which we immediately began. We cleared the subliminal impulses to fall back into the habit. From that point forward, all the healing she had done regarding depression held sway without interference. The clearing also prepared her for full integration of the soul part.

"Helen" did an Ancestral Lines Clearing of the hopeless, helpless, overwhelmed and draining characteristics of the women in her family. Her very powerful power animal was integral in the clearing process. He pulled out of her the strings of those negative characteristics. He also cleared away any connection that would allow the ancestral lines to feed her this negativity from then on.

Helen said this explained why her soul part left at the very early age of one and why another of her soul parts left when she was three because of feeling abandoned by "age one." She said that the revelations from the Ancestral Lines Clearing explained why the females of her family found it hard to be themselves and also why she had miscarried a daughter.

At the end of the clearing, she saw her mother's family lines smiling. Her power animal put spiritual sealing wax on her heart so that she would have no more losses. "Hopeless, helpless, overwhelmed and drained" were replaced by "not-neediness, trust and satisfaction."

This is Flora's outcome of her Ancestral Lines Clearing: *"I wanted to touch base with you, to let you know I feel a deeper calmness and I do not hold onto psychological pain as easily as I once did. I also feel an internal confidence and see a different life for me in my future. I have recognized the strengths in wisdom and understanding not only of myself, but of others. I carry a different love which is fueled by patience and acceptance. My career has been impacted because I see where I should be going, but do not feel irritable or pushed to "make" things happen. I recognize they will happen in their own time and accord. I also have a window opening for a better relationship between my husband and me. I am more accepting of my emotions and validate the wisdom behind the emotions. I am much less reactive to emotional stressors.*

"Windows of guidance seem to come to me now instead of my working so hard to find my path. An example of this is within a week after seeing you, I found a place to start my future which included studying anthropology. I have been working and searching for my niche and a change in careers for such a long while. This suggestion came from deep within, and felt completely right. I opened up a web page search, and found that a nearby college offers courses and degrees within this field. One of the fields includes the cultural anthropology of the area's mountains. My husband received a promotion, which will allow me to pursue a career change in the next few years.

"The changes have been great. I feel a spiritual fulfillment which I seem to have been missing for so long."

Any dysfunctional trait can be cleared from your ancestral lines. When aspects of the following issues are addressed, I often see Spirit leaving the "doorstep" healing gift to millions of people throughout the whole world:

> addictions, creative blocks,
> moroseness, anger, abuse, divisiveness,
> self-doubt, fear, lack of abundance, low self-esteem.

Obviously people everywhere hunger for healing of these issues as well as others not specified in the list directly above. Think of the tens of thousands, even millions, of people genetically connected to each of us from the ancient time of our family origins up to the present! As we do this work for ourselves, we lessen the burden of spiritual growth for other people in the world, known to us or not. In essence, by clearing our family lines of the dysfunction, we are significantly helping the entire human race heal itself.

Chapter Three

Huna

The foremost reason for including basic Huna lore in this book is because my spirit teacher initially told me that Ancestral Lines Clearing is based on Forgiveness and the Huna teachings of the Triune Self. Sharing this understanding with you thus provides a deeper understanding of the Ancestral Lines Clearing process. A secondary yet valuable reason for including it is to show how you and your subconscious can look to Spirit for intuition rather than to "read" the environment. The latter's accuracy is dependent upon each individual's interpretation of emotions, which can be way off base. Spirit, however, gives the "bare bones" truth of a situation. Still another reason for including this material is to help you learn how to pray with greater power and results, while also maintaining strong ethics. All of these reasons involve strengthening your faith in Spirit.

Hawaiian Shamanism

Huna is the Hawaiian form of shamanism. In many ways, it works much like all the other shamanic cultures around the world. All indigenous tribes address spiritual healing, herbal healing, psychic ability, prophecy, creating sacred space, reverence for the earth, honoring all kingdoms in nature (human, animal, plant, mineral), soul retrieval, sending the deceased to the "Light," spirit helpers (power animals, spirit teachers), shamanic journeying, counseling, cosmology, and much more. Some tribes' ceremonies, stories, history and practices may be diametrically opposed to those of some tribes and at the same time remarkably similar to other tribes. Despite the outer physical discrepancies tribal cultures may show us, their shamans all attain similar healing and spiritual results for their people.

In addition, some cultures seem to have specialized in certain facets of shamanic culture. For instance, the Oriental tribes developed sacred space, known as Feng Shui, to an in-depth precise art. The Mayans are famous for their highly developed skills with astronomy, astrology and prophecy. The Hebrews specialized in cosmology, known by them as Kabbalah; it is the history of all creation and contains practices that aid self-understanding, spiritual growth and psychic development. The Hawaiian culture has given us Huna, i.e., a highly developed science of psycho-spirituality.

Max Freedom Long discovered Huna when he researched the hidden meanings within the Hawaiian language. In his writings on Huna he revealed that each of us is a composite of three selves or beings: the Aumakua (ah-oo-mah-<u>koo</u>-ah) is the High Self or Spiritual mind, the uhane (oo-<u>hah</u>-nay) is the middle self or conscious mind, and the unihipili (oo-nih-hih-<u>pee</u>-lee) is the low self or subconscious mind. They are so tightly knit together that they feel and work as one. Each has its own abilities and evolutionary agenda as well as specific duties to the tightly knit trio of the triune self.

The interaction of this triune self can be likened to a tree. <u>The High Self</u> equates to the branches and leaves. It grows ever upward to highest Spirit in its spiritual development, reaches outward to bring in dharmic and karmic service for its two lower selves, and downward to shelter, nurture and protect them. <u>The conscious self</u> equates to the trunk of the tree that supports and creates connection between its two other selves. It receives intuitive guidance from its High Self, keeps the channel open to its subconscious and lovingly commands its subconscious to send prayers up to the High Self. The subconscious self equates to the root system deep into the earth. It provides the energy of positive fluid emotions and feelings to send prayer to the High Self. It can dig deep downward and outward through its library of earth's history, to find what is needed for its other two selves.

For the entire tree of The Triune Self to remain alive to its true calling, all levels require nutrition from grounding application in the earth, regularly taking in the fresh air of Spirit, expressing our uniqueness with the fire of spiritual and emotional fervor, and the spiritual and psychological space to grow outward in life.

The Triune Self's Abilities and Agendas

The High Self is not the same as what some people call the "higher" self. The latter term arose as the result of Freudian psychology talking about the conscious and subconscious minds. It then referred to a more ethical, moral, noble aspect of the self but did not allude to their being a spiritual being as part of it. It is instead the "higher self."

The High Self talked about in Huna is signficantly higher in Spirit than that. It is considered to be the highest Spirit that we can focus on as Mother-Father God, i.e., perfectly balanced male/female energies and highly evolved beyond the human plane that we live in. It is extremely wise, knows everything about you, loves and accepts you unconditionally, answers prayer, protects and guides you. Your personal spirit guides/ power animals/spirit teachers are under its jurisdiction. It is the "head honcho" in matters of ethics, karma and dharma, morality, knowledge of spiritual will, and the path of your soul.

It is high above the head, beyond the twelfth chakra of Monadic divinity that governs ascension, connection to the cosmos and beyond. With your mind's inner vision you may see it as a ball of light or a glow. If you are not visually oriented inwardly, it may show itself to you as a sense of presence or a feeling of emotional warmth or pure knowing that it is there. It conveys a sense of high intelligence and self-awareness.

17

Its evolutionary agenda is unknown to us. However, it does need our offerings of love in order to achieve it, as well as to answer our prayers.

The Hawaiians said that there is also a council of high selves, called the Po'e Aumakua (<u>Poh</u>-eh Ah-oo-mah-<u>koo</u>-ah) that works together for the highest good of all humans whether in a family, a nation, or other grouping. From that, it would seem that the ancient Hawaiians agreed that there is a highest Spirit that many call "God" or that Native Americans call "Great Spirit."

<u>The Middle Self</u> is the one we usually identify with as our conscious self. It is the self that can form words, talk, reason and envision change. It is endowed with free will, i.e., making choices. Think about it: choice is involved in absolutely every moment of life, whether for good or for ill.

It is in charge of guiding the subconscious self and helping it to understand why things happen in life. It can sense higher feelings such as universal love but it can not generate emotions of any kind. (The latter is the low self's ability.) It is largely focused within the head and mind.

Its evolutionary agenda is to learn how to use free will correctly, meaning, in an ethical and moral way that honors and respects everyone including self. It also is to surrender to the High Self's guidance, using its guidance and protection while also balancing that with its own free will and guiding the subconscious self.

<u>The Low Self</u> is the subconscious self and "body mind." It cannot talk, but it can make sounds. It holds the memories of everything you have thought, experienced, heard, seen, felt, smelled, and touched in life whether you remember having done so or not. However, it is unable to discern why things happen.

It can sense the environment (human, nature, spiritual) telepathically. Children who live in an abusive household often develop a "sixth sense" that tells them when it is safe to come home or when to hide from the abuser. That is the telepathic gift of the subconscious in full operation.

The subconscious is the generator of emotions. When you are consumed with an emotion, it is useless to try to override or control it with rational reasoning. Emotions will always override the conscious mind if there is a struggle of control between the two.

This is the self who sends prayers to the High Self. It will also block prayers if it feels guilt or shame. It is focused in the solar plexus, the area of the third chakra. Its evolutionary agenda is to obey the other two selves' instructions as well as to ask the conscious self to tell it the reason for why things happen in life.

Duties of the Triune Self

The High Self. The duties of your High Self are to guide and protect you. It does this through intuitive guidance and warnings, and by reaching out with its high powerful energy to protect you and your aura.

Most of your spirit helpers are of the kingdom of angels; these are messengers from Spirit. If you have personal contact with them, as in channeling or shamanic journeying, you may have noticed that they often have specialized abilities. Therefore it may be more expedient to request help directly from them, much like you would from a department clerk at Sears, rather than going directly to the manager or owner. If you do not have direct contact with them, you can pray to your High Self, and it will send your angels to aid you.

One of your High Self's duties is to answer your prayers, to the extent that you can wield this special spiritual power. If you choose to use it wrongly, it may not answer the prayer. But if it does, it will also set up valuable learning experiences for your future, i.e., karma. These experiences are for the purpose of helping you to learn how to be a better channel for Spirit and to better understand how to work with other humans and all of nature. When you learn what it intends you to learn, the joys and benefits of dharma become more noticeable. Dharma may be most evident through the joys, good luck and other benefits you receive in life. It may also be evident through greater clarity in the intuitive guidance your High Self sends you or from miraculous escapes from danger.

The conscious self's duties are to learn how to follow the intuitive direction of your High Self and to oversee the education of your subconscious.

Every choice you make in life has a reason behind it, whether that reason is valid or not, ethical or not. Following the input from your High Self helps you learn how to make right choices.

Answering the "why?" questions from your subconscious, to the best of your ability, helps your emotions and thoughts stay in better balance. If you do not know to do this, or otherwise shun responsibility, the subconscious will bring its own peculiar reasoning to a circumstance. It will link emotions, beliefs and events in an illogical way. That is called a renegade memory and is stored in your spiritual library of life experiences. The renegade memory is a block to healing and manifests as irrational thinking and beliefs, or explosions of emotion without knowing why, or at worst, psycho-spiritual causes behind illness.

For example: *Many years ago I visited friends in Buffalo, NY, over the July Fourth holiday. That day we picnicked in their backyard. We adults were busy chatting. One of the children, a three-year-old girl, sat on the grass near the picnic table, completely engrossed in petting her little dog. Her mother told me that the dog went everywhere with her, even into the bathtub; the two were inseparable. Moments later, someone in the next yard set off a volley of loud fireworks. The little girl screamed and cried hysterically. It took her parents close to a half hour to calm her down. After that, everytime she looked at her dog she started screaming in terror once again. This continued to happen to the point that several weeks later her parents had to give the dog away. They were saddened to have to do this, but there was no other recourse. Even after giving the pet away, she still cried in terror at the sight of any other dog.*

Obviously, the dog did not create the loud sound that terrified her so. Prior to the traumatic sound, she had been engrossed in the emotions of love for her pet. Her subconscious instantly transferred her emotional attention from love of the dog to terror of the explosive-sounds. That plus her eyes being fixated on the dog allowed her subconscious to illogically pair the sound with the dog. And voila! A renegade memory of "the dog caused the terror" was planted deep in her mind.

I have no idea how this now-a-woman has fared with the phobia of dogs. If she tried to search her memories she would not find a memory of a dog that truly threatened her. Her path to healing would be blocked until such point that she could recall, realize and minutely separate the events logically regarding that day.

Another part of guiding the subconscious is to ask it, with love and firmness, to keep its energies focused inward towards its conscious mind and High Self. Part of this obedience is to help you recall anything in its library of life memories. For instance, you can ask it to recall where you left your car keys or remember information for a test or keep focused on a song you are performing at a concert or to send a prayer to the High Self. In all cases, it is important to be respectful, strong and caring, and always praise it for a job well done. This right relationship creates an atmosphere of love and trust within you, such that your subconscious will willingly divulge fears and sources of blocks, and reduce shame and guilt. Keep in mind as well, that if there is ever a difference of opinion between you and your High Self, the subconscious will side with the High Self in most instances.

The subconscious self uses emotions to help you know what is going on in the library of your memories, beliefs and attitudes. But it can not reason nor envision anything new beyond what it currently feels and sees. Turbulent emotions point to one of your issues or to a renegade memory. If the subconscious has made a renegade memory, it knows it. It will feel shame or guilt that it has done something it is not designed to do. However, there is a difference between feeling guilty because you know you have done something wrong or are carrying a grudge, and feeling guilty as "par for the course." The latter tends to indicate a renegade memory.

The conscious self cannot send a prayer under its own power; it must always go through the subconscious. Guilt and shame cause the subconscious to refuse to send up prayer. It also blocks prayer if it knows that you are harboring a grudge towards someone. If you carry any grudges, forgiveness is crucial, to unblock the path. When this is done and you feel relief from it, you can command the subconscious to send love up to the High Self and it will happen.

Developing Rapport, Focus and Protection

All of the following exercises are included for the primary purpose of helping you develop the rapport and focus necessary for working effectively with your High Self in doing your own Ancestral Lines Clearing.

"Sticky Side In, Slippery Side Out." In Huna studies it is generally known that the subconscious has both a sticky and a slippery trait. The slippery side, when it is turned inward, is like thinking to do or say something one moment and then a split second later the thought is gone and you cannot get it back. Obviously that is not a helpful use for this aspect of your subconscious.

The sticky side, turned outward, applies to invisible tendrils the subconscious can send out to anything or anyone. My Huna instructor said he could do this with wrapped Christmas presents, finding out what is inside; his family seldom could surprise him. I use my sticky-side outward when I boil eggs for breakfast. I do not use a timer. I merely set the intention "is the egg cooked the way I like it, i.e., yolk soft and white hard?" Then I look at the egg, let my mind go into an off-focus mode (sort of like the feeling of day-dreaming) and allow the truth to show up in my mind. I know immediately whether the white is hard or still runny, or if the entire egg is hard. When I crack it open it is indeed as the pictured answer that had come to mind. That picture was put there by my subconscious.

These are helpful abilities when done consciously. The problem arises when it becomes a habit, meaning, out of conscious control. Such a habit can create a strong focus on relying upon other people and outer authority to govern your life, i.e., co-dependency. True spiritual focus is to rely on Spirit, not on people. Spirit is the one who gave you your soul and your soul's mission in life. Other people do not have that knowledge nor access to your akashic records. When your subconscious reaches out to others out of habit, its tendrils can pick up anything anywhere, and all of a sudden you are picking up an emotion from someone else and taking it on as your own, or picking up a cold or illness from someone else. Someone else can reach out and control you through attaching their tendrils to yours, much like the analogy of grabbing your out-stretched hand and pulling you in any direction they want. Obviously, this is not a helpful use for this aspect of your subconscious.

Spiritual Protection. In 2008, my spirit teacher in the upper world taught me how to work with the sticky and slippery aspects in a way that addresses the desirable uses of both. I call it "sticky side in, slippery side out" because of the way it helps you remember, pray, and protect yourself against someone else's invasive energy.

Think of your subconscious as a ball enveloping the middle of your torso. Is the outside of that ball sticky or slippery? If the outside is slippery, then the inside has to be sticky. This is the positive use of those aspects. In this position, you can think for yourself, are impervious to others' attempts to control you, and you can feel more centered and at peace. Here is what Cara, one of my students, told me several weeks after a workshop:

"I am working on coming to terms with my empathic nature and how it is for my highest good rather than a problem and a handicap. The 'sticky side in' mode has been a significant factor in my journey. I continue to be blown away at its ability to get me centered immediately. When I can't get centered using it, I know I've got someone else's stuff in my auric field. Truly, truly profound. I'm trying to train myself that 'sticky side in' is my 'energetic posture' and merging with the greater field of collective consciousness is done on command rather than the other way around."

If the outside of the subconscious ball is sticky, then the inside has to be slippery. In this position you can be easily manipulated by others, have trouble thinking for yourself, have difficulty remembering things, and take on stuff from others. This is the negative use of those two aspects. It is quite simple to turn your sticky side in.

1. Reflect inward with a focus on your subconscious.

2. Firmly, respectfully and with love, command it to turn the sticky side in and the slippery side out.

3. Know that the action is both right and safe. If you feel a slight shudder of fear, apprehension or nausea, reaffirm to your subconscious that this is the right thing to do and that it is indeed safe.

4. When the reversal of the sides occurs completely, you will notice a difference. It should feel safer.

5. Express appreciation to your subconscious for having faith in your guidance.

6. Sit in that feeling a while, to feel the newness of it.

Inner Rapport
1. When your stick side has turned firmly inward, ask your subconscious to turn its tendrils up to your conscious mind.
2. Let it know that you will answer and clarify any questions it has about the meaning of life's circumstances.
3. If at any time you do not know the reason, just tell it you do not know and that it is ok to not know. Not everything in life is explainable.
4. Your sincerity about that will help your subconscious feel that it does not have to make a renegade memory.
5. At any time in the future when you are ready, ask your subconscious to turn its tendrils up to your High Self.
6. Completion of that feels like you are more centered or tuned in to Spirit. Sit a while with this focused intention.
7. Do not expect any visualizations, although sometimes that does happen. The main purpose here is to become more in tune with Spirit.

Meditation. In the inner rapport section, you learned a simple yet effective form of meditation! It takes only five minutes a day. Any time during the day that you find your sticky side is out again, just turn it inward. Each time, rest in that for a few minutes to re-center yourself. In this way you are more protected from outer energies and more focused on Spirit. Fun, yes? It is what some gurus say "learning how to live your whole life in a state of meditation."

Meditation is considered to be a companion to prayer. It is said that prayer is talking to God and meditation is listening for God's answer. Some forms of meditation are strictly for relaxation, others for calming the mind of its chatter, some for insight into mental patterns that do not serve you constructively, and some for alignment with Spirit's higher purposes and awareness. What I am teaching you here is the latter. It is the preamble for the kind of attunement and prayer that is needed for working effectively with your High Self in Ancestral Lines Clearing. However, if you find another form of meditation or of "centering prayer" that is more helpful to you, by all means go with that. What I am sharing here is only one of many possibilities.

As you meditate on a daily basis, just keep the focus and do not expect any results. Be open to them, yes, but do not judge "success" by whether you experience results in any given session. There will be changes deep inside you long before anything will be felt at the outer more recognizable levels. Over time you will be able to look back on months of daily meditation and realize what has changed for you. (Some commonly reported changes are more calmness or an improved attitude or a more beneficial state of mind during your daily activities, or easier coping ability.) After doing that first form of meditation on a daily basis for several weeks, your conscious and subconscious minds will be accustomed to it. The next stage may then be appropriate:

1. Think of your subconscious self being focused in your heart chakra and your conscious self being focused in your head.
2. Know that your heart and head are connected.
3. Now focus on your High Self.
4. Let your subconscious and conscious awareness rise up to it and become one with it.
5. Rest in that for five minutes a day. This meditation is in place of the previous one.
6. If at any time you prefer that previous stage, by all means do it. It is perfectly fine to go back for a review or to alternate the styles of meditation you do.

Spiritual Attunement and Cleansing

A primary reason for my including the next two exercises is that in doing them you give your will freely to your High Self. Meaning, you are teaching yourself how to let Spirit guide your life. A regular practice of meditation, prayer and spiritual cleansing is an excellent way to become more in tune with your High Self and its highest purposes, and to be guided rightly. Ability to get results from prayer is crucial for doing an Ancestral Lines Clearing on your own.

After a week or two of doing the heart chakra exercise you can add a Spiritual Attunement component. Here is one:

1. First focus on the High Self for a few minutes.
2. Ask it to shed its light down through you and around you.
3. When you feel that that the High Self's light is fully in place, ask it to attune you to its pure vibration.
4. Be totally receptive and trusting. It may feel like being aware of your entire being and your High Self all at once.

Or it may feel like you are holding space within every part of your being.

5. Allow your High Self to do anything it knows needs to be done to cleanse your aura.

6. Sit in that for five minutes a day either before or after meditation.

The Spiritual Cleansing meditation is a slight variation on the attunement one.

1. Be sure your sticky side is in.

2. Command your subconscious to connect its tendrils to your High Self.

3. Ask that great being to surround you and fill you with its strongest cleansing vibration.

4. Sit in this for five minutes, all the while allowing your High Self to do what it knows is beneficial for you. At first, the energy may feel slightly different than the attunement one.

5. The effect may be very subtle and gentle, or sometimes quite strong.

6. As you continue to use it, the scope of what it can cleanse will deepen.

Like other disciplines in spiritual life, the cleansing ability will take time to develop. It will remove other people's tendrils and energy from your aura, thus protecting you from their influence. That is valuable protection, but it is not intended to take the place of shielding visualizations you may use for other purposes.

Prayer

At any point in the meditation process, you can send love to your High Self. Sending love to the High Self builds spiritual connection, gives more power and energy to the High Self to do what it needs to do for its own evolution and for you, and builds your ability to pray.

You know your subconscious self is fully involved if you feel the love going up. If you do not feel it going up, then continue any of the above stages of meditation. Also check to see if you need to forgive or accept forgiveness from anyone.

You can test the prayer process again after a while. Understand: this takes time. With daily diligence, it will become a satisfying pattern.

Q & A
This question and answer section brings a few of the above teachings together for clarity on how the Triune Self's duties relate to your life.

• What are some signals that your sticky side is out?

You cannot think nor make decisions well....You are overly vulnerable to outer influences....You have difficulty sending prayers up to your High Self....You worry.

When you worry you do not rely on your High Self. Instead, you rely strictly on your conscious mind, wondering what will happen. To rectify this, merely command your subconscious to send your worries, fears, pain and troubles up to your High Self. It will transmute that negative energy to pure light, which is one of its duties to you. Just turn it over to Spirit. "Let Go and Let God." Act where and when you can, yes, but in your thoughts and emotions turn it over to Spirit.

• What patterns can cause "sticky side out"?

Fear. Habit. Trauma. Worry.

• How does the power of love help you?

When the conscious and subconscious selves send love to the High Self, that great being builds your manifestation ability and intuitive guidance.

When the conscious self sends love to the subconscious self, better inner guidance and rationality result.

When the subconscious self sends love to the conscious self, feelings of peace and less fear pervade your being.

• Why is listening to yourself important?

When you listen to your High Self, there is deepening within, more meaning and greater interest in life. The same is true when the subconscious and conscious selves listen to each other. All of this keeps you more in tune to the true unique self that you are.

Chapter Four

Ho'oponopono aka Forgiveness

Forgiveness is the process of psychologically and spiritually letting go of the past and releasing someone from the harm they caused you, whether perceived or real. You stop mentally and emotionally trying to redo the past. You give it up so that the past does not hold you hostage. Forgiveness is a process of "letting go and letting God" deal with the issue you have with the other person, or even with yourself! It lifts the load of pain off your shoulders, making your path lighter, and letting you know you have a second chance at happiness. You are doing this for you, not for someone else. It is a process of letting go of attachments of any kind that make you feel bad about yourself or anyone else.

Forgiveness in no way condones or dismisses a person's actions. It does not say that what was done is right. It just leaves it in Spirit's hands. Connie Newton, a former teacher of mine, once said to 400 of us at a conference that "carrying a grudge is like saying to God that you want to be in charge of that person's karma. But if you give the grudge up to God, their karma will come to them a lot swifter than if you continue to hold onto it. However, if wanting them to get their karma more swiftly is your only reason for giving up the grudge, you still are not forgiving them." The point is, forgiveness includes letting go of any negative feelings you have toward the other person. Besides, no human truly knows what another person's spirit needs. It is not ours to judge. Only Spirit can know what that person needs, to mend their ways: a kick in the pants, a hug, or something else.

The counseling field generally recognizes that sometimes a person can forgive too soon and should not be pressured to forgive until ready. This is true when you are not being honest about your feelings towards the other person or have not yet uncovered everything that needs healing. Forgiving too soon could evoke feelings of unwarranted guilt, feeling less worthy, feeling shameful or angry. All of those "down" feelings hamper the healing process.

On the other hand, if you are well aware of how you feel regarding a specific event, then forgiveness is very much in order even if it is just for one small incident. True forgiveness frees you and makes you feel more whole, more worthy, more optimistic, more peaceful. In addition, after you forgive the person, you do not have to feel love for them, nor even like them. In fact, you can choose to never again associate with them.

A friend of mine used to respond with "Ahh, it never happened" any time someone apologized to him. He was a very easy-going, congenial person. Then one day a relative did something that deeply hurt his feelings. He could not get over it for years. I finally asked him why he could not forgive, and he responded "because it happened!" Forgiveness does not infer that the incident never happened. It did!

Right Or Wrong?

When you forgive, you still have your conscience to tell you when something is wrong. Forgiveness frees up your psychic antenna for truth, such as the ability to discern who or what to trust and who or what not to trust. Not forgiving clouds that antenna and you feel like you can trust no one. In other words, not forgiving makes you project wrongs where there may be no wrong. If you hold a grudge for a long time, you end up projecting onto everyone the animosity you really feel toward one person. What that person did to you occurred within a limited amount of time. Even if it was a horrendous repeated action during childhood, it is still confined to your childhood years. By not forgiving them, you are continuing to hurt yourself every minute of every hour of every day since then. You are doing yourself more harm, in a more continuous way, than they ever did to you! It is now *you* who are hurting you! That is self abuse.

Here is what "Cara", one of my clients, was told by her spirit teacher during a soul integration session:

"Forgiveness is easy, once learned; you have just forgotten how. Hurt is an illusion the mind attaches to. Freeing the mind of illusions allows natural forgiveness. You do not trust the forgiveness process. You think they might do it again, if you forgive. Trusting is a matter of the heart. Trust your heart and you will release grudges."

Not forgiving someone brings more of the same treatment into your life...if not from the same person, then from others who are like them. Paradoxically, forgiveness will stop further occurrences of that treatment! It cuts the cords that tie you to that person and the past.

To illustrate, bring to mind a hypothetical image of two people called "Peggy" and her brother "Joe". Imagine they are very angry with each other. The angry emotional ties between them look, at a psychic level, like ropes tying them securely together. Everywhere she moves, she angrily jerks his rope and he yanks hers. The emotional charge is a constant reminder of his influence in her life. Sometimes the jerk pulls her to him in face-to-face confrontation. Sometimes they are far apart, neither thinking about the other. However, the angry rope stretching tightly between them causes another person, "Bill", to trip. He senses her anger and ends up coming at Peggy with the same animosity that Joe does.

Now picture Peggy forgiving Joe, and letting go of the ropes. No longer can he pull her to him. She is free of him. She feels lighter, with less emotional pull on her, and she hardly thinks of him anymore. She also is no longer dragging around the anger rope that would make Bill trip. Bill senses this at the non-verbal level, if not consciously, and is more carefree and congenial in her presence.

Part of this process is recognizing that everyone is human and therefore fallible. We all make mistakes: you, me, them. It is such a relief to be able to release all of that and get on with true living!

How It Feels

Regardless of how you feel, if your thoughts or Spirit says you need to forgive, then defer to that wisdom. Even if you still want to hold onto blame and hard feelings, at least try the process. You may be astonished at how you feel afterwards. Forgiveness works if you use it. You do not have to feel ready for it. You do not have to feel like you need to resolve things first, nor to get the other person to ask for forgiveness.

For example, *there was one time when I was very angry at someone for something they said to me. I really felt like calling them up and "telling them off." I envisioned how justifying that would feel. Yet, a small "prompting" memory arose of how peaceful I had felt at previous times when I had forgiven someone. The "justifying" feeling felt minuscule in comparison to the power of "peace," so I chose to do the Ho'oponopono ritual despite how my emotions felt. I summoned up all the courage, fortitude and sincerity I could, and went ahead with the very ritual you see in the script later in this chapter. By the time I reached the end of it, amazingly I felt like it was time to forgive the person! Peace prevailed.*

Intention is more important than feelings. That is because intention comes from a spiritual level, which influences the lower vibrational levels of the mind and emotions. If your spirit and intention know you are going to forgive, your emotions are compelled to follow suit.

Huna Ho'oponopono

As stated in the Introduction, Ancestral Lines Clearing is based on the Huna "Ho'oponopono" ritual of forgiveness. Even though cultures throughout the world are aware of forgiveness, it appears that the Hawaiians developed it in a highly specialized way. They used it in the presence of all parties involved in a personal infraction with a member of their tribe. The Kahuna (shaman) kept their dialogue going until everyone present was comfortable with the outcome, whether that took one hour or many days. The Ho'oponopono rite was used at pertinent stages throughout.

When I was in metaphysical seminary, one of my professors and his wife conducted a class on pastoral counseling. They had reworked the Ho'oponopono into a script that could be used in absentia. Its effectiveness is supported by Spirit, meaning that Spirit takes the position of proxy for the humans involved, whether alive or dead. I found this very comforting, because forgiveness in person at times can lead to misunderstandings and sometimes can cause problems or make problems worse. With Spirit as proxy, the ties are released from our end, which frees us. The ties may be released from the other person's end only if that person chooses it; Spirit gives each of us our free will.

In this ritual, you are working at spiritual levels within. In no way are you interfering with the other person's free will, if you follow the instructions regarding their light. You can call on highest Spirit to aid you at any time. The method can be done at any level of consciousness, whether in trance or waking reality. The only requirement is a strong intention to forgive and release the other person.

A forgiveness practice will keep you from accumulating negativity that leads to karmic debt. It will keep a negative trait from distorting your family's DNA. Even if you are not ready for Ancestral Lines Clearing, you will still get immediate benefit from this chapter and the one on Huna. Inner growth and healing tends to go in layers. You will progress as you are ready. You do not have to be perfect to find this helpful.

Ho'oponopono Script

You can reword the following script to suit you; as written here, it is merely a starting point. If the word "forgiveness" is uncomfortable to you, try substituting it with other like-minded words such as "release," "let go let God," or "let it go." You can reword it to fit your individual need, such as: releasing the hurts of the past or forgiving self, circumstances, emotions, or the planet.

In the italicized script below, pause at each pattern of dots, to fully feel the effects of what you request; move on when ready.

Begin by imagining your connection to your High Self. For instance: you may see the High Self as a globe of bright white light above your head, or as a glow of light right above the crown of your head. If you do not "see," maybe you feel a warmth, or sense the presence of that great spiritual being or just know you are connected to it. Each person uses different inner senses. Translate my "seeing" words to whatever works for you.

Picture the other person at a comfortable distance from you, permeated and surrounded by the light of their own choosing. Do not tamper with their light.

Notice the connection between the two of you

> **Inwardly say to this person as sincerely as possible**
> "I, (your name), forgive you, (other person's name),
> for all the hurts, both real and imagined...
> known and unknown... intentional and unintentional...
> that you have done to me from the beginning of time to the
> present....And I release you from all of these."

Notice the ties dropping away. Allow the release until all ties fall off that are going to. Fill your vacated spaces with the bright spiritual light of the High self, asking it for reinforcement.

> **Inwardly say to the person as sincerely as possible**
> "I accept your forgiveness of me for all the hurts,
> both real and imagined...known and unknown...
> intentional and unintentional...
> that I have done to you from the beginning of time to the
> present....And I accept your release of me for all of these."

Notice more ties dropping away. Do nothing to that person's ties nor energy. Allow the release until all ties fall off that are going to. If not all of them go, repeat the above process.

At any time during the ritual you can fill your vacated spaces with the bright spiritual light of the High self, asking it for reinforcement. Do nothing with any vacated spaces that may occur in the other person!

Interestingly, the other person will leave the scene spontaneously when their Spirit knows that all is forgiven. Notice the relief and joy within you.

Notice, During This Process:

The underlined words in the script are very important. It is not possible to require another person to forgive you. However, you can accept their forgiveness if or when it happens. The very act of accepting it now allows ties to release at your end, if not at theirs. If that person wants to keep dragging around their heavy ties, that is their business. At least you are free of your end of it.

Notice images, thoughts or realizations that may occur. They may give you deeper understanding into the nature of the relationship and how it has affected you.

Does the relationship seem to be one-sided? That is, does the other person not wish to forgive you? You may have to forgive the same person more than once, especially if there has been a lot of emotional interaction. That is OK. Having to forgive them again does not mean that the past forgiveness has been undone. It only means that a new layer of relationship has surfaced.

Do you continue to feel energy coming at you from that person? You may find it important to ask your High Self to shield you in white light or a blue egg of light, or in some other way protect you spiritually when around them or when thoughts occur regarding them. You may also find it important to do this forgiveness exercise each time as well.

Do you feel pulled toward the other person? Immediately fill yourself with light from your High Self. What you released in the forgiveness process may have occupied a major part of your being, thus leaving a spiritual hole within you. This is particularly true if you notice bland darkness or sense emptiness within you after releasing. The vacated attachments have left a vacuum. Nature abhors a vacuum and tends to fill it with anything that is close at hand. That is why you are being drawn to that person: you have been accustomed to filling yourself up with them, strange as it may sound. Instead, ask your High Self to fill you with Its Light. Also continue to do both parts of this method, asking your High Self to help you disconnect from the other person.

Ancestral Lines Clearing and Forgiveness

If an Ancestral Lines Clearing could be done strictly through the use of the Ho'oponopono as above, anytime you forgive someone it would instantly change the DNA. It does not do so. However, by forgiving people as a natural rule of thumb, in this life, you do keep your DNA in better shape for the future. A forgiveness practice is needed in anongoing manner to keep your DNA from being altered negatively.

You probably will discover that while doing one-on-one forgiveness of people, you intuitively become aware of why another person may have been carrying hard feelings towards you. I was shocked the first time that occurred with me. Here is a long-remembered occurrance of this:

My school music administrator had approached me in the faculty room and gently talked with me about some incident regarding the musical we were rehearsing with faculty and students. I sensed an under current of dissatisfaction coming from him even though his face and voice were gentle. I could not for the life of me figure out what he was talking about. After he left the room, I just dismissed the whole experience and shrugged it off.

That subsequent summer while visiting my Dad, I sat out on his front deck practicing the forgiveness ritual during the hour that he took a nap. One of the people who popped to my head was the school's music administrator and that very encounter in the faculty room. As soon as I acknowledged the image my subconscious gave me, I did the Ho'oponopono to him. At the end of it I suddenly realized that he had thought I was the person who had erred. It was actually someone else!

It may seem strange that you could possibly get detailed pertinent information about the other person, even something you had never been aware of before. However, the spiritual cords connecting the two of you are part of the subconscious's telepathic ability. Apparantly, Spirit allows those cords to hold information that would heal the relationship between you. What a gift!

Chapter Five

High Energies Needed

Getting Results

When my Spirit Teacher gave me the Ancestral Lines Clearing process, it felt very easy to use. So easy, in fact, that I thought anyone could use it. Initially I did it during a shamanic journey. Later on I found it could be done in other forms of trance. The clients and workshop students to whom I taught it also found good results. Then I started noticing that some people in subsequent workshops had a bright energetic response to the forgiveness exercise, but a dull look took over their eyes regarding the rest of it. The dull look told me they had no success with the process. Some even said they had spaced out.

As a result, I instituted a pre-requisite of shamanic journeying for future workshops, including one large conference whose attendees all knew how to do shamanic journeying. But again some of the students evidenced little to no success, while others gravitated to it with enthusiastic and immediate results. During this same period I encountered several people who succeeded in the process even though they did not know how to journey. Each said they had the ability to pray and receive results from it. From that I realized that journeying alone is not the success factor with this work; ability to get results from prayer is. Those who can call in the help of high-powered spirit guides or Archangels quite naturally have the ability to get results from prayer. To succeed in clearing ancestral lines, a person needs to be able to channel high-powered energy from Spirit, or to call in spirit guides who can wield high-powered healing energy. Spirit responds to the prayer call from the human.

Aura Cleansing

In the mid-2000 decade, I began to do Aura Cleansing with Archangels Michael and Raphael. Calling them in to do cleansing work feels quite similar to calling in my own High Self. Both ways are a form of prayer, albeit a very specialized and high-powered form. Aura Cleansing is a high powered form of depossession which transmutes or clears detrimental energy from the aura. This energy can be emotional detritus; enmeshed energy, soul parts or controls from other humans; earth-bound spirits; demons, high dark Archangels and more. As these detrimental energies leave, clients immediately feel the release, a lightness in their aura, improved clarity of thought, and/or spontaneous insights of how to improve their spiritual growth and life.

An important part of an aura cleansing session is to also bring healing to those areas of the body where cleansing occurred. Archangel Raphael does that for my clients. He may bring in soothing energy, or heal a realign chakras or help the mind adjust to more functional beliefs (personal, not religious).

The aura cleansing and healing is done by these great spiritual beings and their accompanying angels with the use of very high-powered light. My purpose is to keenly observe them and keep the intention. What they do is always what they know the client needs, and they do it quickly. As I progressed in ability to maintain the required focus, the Archangels began incorporating others of my modalities as needed for a client's healing. For example: an occasional soul retrieval or helping a person integrate a soul part already there; extraction of an illness or clearing buildups of negative emotion; changing dysfunctional beliefs to functional ones; clearing and reconstructing chakras. From time to time they have also brought in forms of healing I had not known of before.

Archangel Michael has helped significantly with past-lives. At times this comes as a suggestion that my client visit a specific past-life to gain understanding and healing. On other occasions he transmutes some past-lives with a burst of light without giving details of the life. He says that the client already has that information and all that is needed is to remove old energy patterns that played into problems. He began clearing ancestral lines in much the same way as past-lives, i.e., sometimes giving details and sometimes not. (Ancestral Lines Clearing has occurred during soul retrievals as well as in aura cleansing.)

High Powered Spiritual Energies

Ancestral Lines Clearing requires Spirit's high vibrations of the Light in order to transmute or remove detrimental aspects of an ancestral line's DNA so that it leads the family to a better destiny. In some cases the transmutation seems to change the fabric of time to create a new time line that is more positive...as if previous generations suddenly "woke up" to understanding there is a better way of doing things. In other cases, the detrimental aspects are removed completely from the DNA, leaving only the pure and uplifting aspects in place. With both of these, it is as if a "river of forgetfulness" flows through the family lines, letting family members automatically think and behave in new and constructive ways, like "Gina's" cousin (chapter two) being given a gift of grace.

In Ancestral Lines Clearing, Spirit uses the high-powered energy to remove or transmute the detrimental trait from the family DNA. Essentially, it is a form of spiritual surgery. All spiritual power is vibration. In our mind's eye it tends to show up in some form of the "four elements" of fire, water, air and earth. If your High Self says it will use water to clear your ancestral lines, it obviously does not refer to a small pond because there is little to no movement in such a body of water. As *water* the high vibration may show up as a tsunami, water fall, typhoon or a torrential river. As *fire* it may show up as a brilliant beam of light, laser-light, electricity or a blow torch of fire. As *air* it may be like a tornado or cyclone, a hurricane, a high-pitched piercing or low-pitched thunderous sound. As *earth* it may be like an earthquake or clods of soil falling off the family lines. These elements can also be paired together to form an even more powerful force. For example: earth and fire can become lava, wind and dry earth can become an overpowering sandstorm, fire and water can serve the dual purpose of burning up dysfunctional DNA fragments followed by water soothing the lines.

The key here is to ask your High Self for the highest most powerful form of whatever element it knows will best clear the lines. (Be sure to allow your High Self to make the choice, rather than you. If you choose it, and it is not the same as what the High Self knows is right, the element will not be powerful enough to clear the lines.) As the image of that element or combination of elements is shown to you, pay close attention to what senses or aspects of senses you are using to perceive them. You may discover that several work together. The more senses active at the same time, the easier it is to stay in the focussed trance that best facilitates the clearing.

For instance: When I do clearing for someone else, I frequently hear a distant explosion while also seeing a white laser light. One of my students reported a howling wind while the lines were being cleared and the sound of water gently lapping at the shoreline when it was completed. Another student saw the image of a sand storm engulfing an entire city; the image provoked a much greater sense of power than just reading or hearing the words "sand storm."

Your High Self will bring to your awareness whatever combination of senses that will best help you know how to follow its clearing. It is imperative to the clearing process that you be constantly aware of what is going on; that is why I suggested above that you look for multiple senses active at the same time. If you allow your mind to wander, you are choosing to stop the process. Spirit will recognize your lack of will or readiness to do this work. As you stay engaged with it, you continuously give permission for it to do the work. Your engaged free will allows your High Self to do the clearing.

Note: If you are unable to call in the requisite powerful energy, you can contact an energy worker to do it for you. Use the information and insights above to assess whether an energy worker can help you or not. Even so, when you enlist an energy worker to do your Ancestral Lines Clearing, it is imperative that you stay present and focused, for it to truly work. Your focus on truth, willingness to face the unknown, and being receptive are just as important for success as is your energy worker's ability to call in high-powered spiritual energy.

Forms of Energy Work

There are numerous energy work modalities prevalent in our current culture. Reiki and Touch For Health are probably the most well-known as being reliably beneficial. They transmit universal life force energy into you and in so doing, a relaxed glow of love replaces whatever is troubling your mind and body. They aid your self esteem and self love, which are major boosts to your immune system on all levels. They are highly beneficial in speeding up your healing. Crucial, in fact. They can be likened to internal medicine and to Archangel Raphael's gentle, nurturing, healing energy that helps restore areas of your energy that have been wounded. Ancestral Lines Clearing can be likened to surgery and to Archangel Michael's excising or removal of detrimental energies. These are two dramatically different kinds of healing modalities. No mistake about it: all are powerful forms of healing. However, the way Reiki and Touch for Health are done is not designed to excise negative energy. That is not their purpose. They do not have the capacity to clear the ancestral lines.

The High Self, Archangel Michael and sometimes the Christ Light have been known to do major clearing work. There are also other Archangels of the Light who help. Each energy practitioner may call on Archangels of different names. If you are researching energy workers to do the Ancestral Lines Clearing for you, it is best to ask if they do surgical-style clearing or restorative healing. The former will clear the lines; the latter will not.

Mindsets for Working with Spirit

Prayer. As stated before, you can do this work comparatively easily if you consistently get results from prayer. Prayer with only words is like going up an eight-foot ladder; it gets you only so far, then nothing more. Intuition may realize something is higher, but if that is based strictly on emotions or thinking, then you are using only your own energy rather than accessing Spirit's energy. With Ancestral Lines Clearing you must access Spirit's energy. When you do, it is Spirit that takes the initiative and does the work; you do not.

Powerful prayer means that the powerful energy of your High Self or Archangel Michael is easily accessible to you, and your mind is clear and focused so that you can stay conscious to what is happening with its powerful clearing. It is still Spirit that does the work, not you. In other words, prayer energy, not prayer words, gets the work done. We humans do not know how to do what the Archangels do. We can go through the motions, yes, but get results, no. We can see details but seeing details does not make changes. Only spirit and its energy can do that.

Whether an energy-worker channels high-powered healing energies through them or instead chooses to watch the Archangels or Spirit heal you, the results are similar. It is still Spirit doing the work, not us humans. Yet we are partners in the healing process. We humans need to be unconditionally receptive to the healing energies of Spirit. That means wanting the truth no matter how it shows up. It also means not trying to help nor block what the energies may do.

Worrying. Ironically, one signal that you may have the ability to get results from prayer is a negative one. Meaning, that you worry a lot, to the extent that what you worry about actually comes true. Some people say that worrying is a negative form of prayer. Others say that it is the absence of prayer. I think that both statements are true. The profound difference between them is whether what you worry about actually comes true. If you can worry something into reality, you can also pray positive results into reality.

To overcome this habitual tendency, focus intently on your thoughts and feelings for the next week or two. Each time you find yourself worrying, look at what you are worrying about. Then send up a prayer, asking for the positive results of that subject. Work to use positive prayer and let go of worry. (Ethically, be sure you are not infringing upon someone else's free will in the matter...whether positively or negatively. If it is a specific matter, ask that person for permission to pray for them or send healing.)

Truth. Wanting the truth is more important than any other attitude when working with the Archangels. This "truth focus" must be from both the healer and the client. It has to transcend petty whims, wanting to do the work yourself, wanting it to be done in a certain way, expecting it to show up in a certain experiential way or order, or wanting your agenda to be adhered to. It means allowing Spirit to determine the course of action, where to work, how to do the work, how long it will take, and whether it is already known or completely unknown. Both the client and the healer must have this intention in order for Spirit to work. If either does not, the energy stalls. The archangels deem human free will to be paramount; therefore, your will must align with the truth for this work to be complete.

For example: *At the beginning of one session, I told my client to just be open and receptive to what the energy is doing. When I started my trance I saw the usual scene for healing: a platform in space with him lying on it. Archangel Michael stood on the other side of the platform from where I was perched. He began sending Light to clear my client's aura, but the healing stopped almost as soon as it started. I moved to a place inwardly that Archangel Michael often has me go to when I want to make sure that I am not the one who is interfering with the healing. Again Michael sent light and again the healing stopped shortly after.*

At that point I opened my eyes and told my client briefly that the Archangel kept stopping his work. I asked him what his experience was. He said, "Well, I did as you told me to do: be open. So I was opening my chakras." I assured him that his intention was noble, but opening up his chakras was his human will interfering. That was why Archangel Michael stopped sending light; he deemed my client's free will to be more important than sending healing. In other words, my client was unwittingly interfering with what Archangel Michael knew needed to happen. I asked him to not open his chakras this time and instead just be receptive and observant. As I went back into trance, Michael and his angels immediately began the clearing and healing. This time they continued for quite a while with no glitch.

It is possible to think you want the truth but something inside may resist, misunderstand or interfere. No blame here. We all have instances of that. It is just the way growth and healing work, at times. Spirit honors your free will and does not want you to be pushed beyond your capacity to endure. It will do everything possible to help you heal, to the extent that you allow it. Your free will is paramount; you can stop the process at any time.

Think of "truth" as being linked with allowing the unknown to appear. It is a focus of awareness, not just saying to yourself over and over that you want the truth. Yes, at first you may need to state the words, "I want the truth no matter how it shows up, whether known or unknown, whether it is what I expect or not." After saying that, keep it as an unspoken intention that carries no words in your thoughts. Some people describe their experience as merely a feeling of truth, or a feeling of purity of purpose. Just be receptive to whatever comes up.

Faith. A frame of mind equal to wanting the truth is faith in Spirit. Faith that Spirit knows what is right and faith that what it does will indeed produce beneficial and healing results. This is paramount. Faith replaces any doubt or fear, whether it is self-doubt or fear of astral vibes or anything else in your pattern of issues. Part of the "truth focus" is being willing to do what it takes to help yourself or your client while at the same time having the faith that Spirit would not do anything that would be detrimental to you or your client.

Chapter Six

Preparation for the Work

Before Beginning

Before beginning an Ancestral Lines Clearing, present to your High Self several issues that you have already been working to heal. If you have not worked on given issues, delete them from your list. No matter how small a piece of that untapped issue you would choose, it may still overwhelm you during the clearing process. You would be disappointed with the results because it would seem like nothing had been done. This is because the Ancestral Lines Clearing clears only the ancestral lines, not your personal work. If you have any personal karma related to the issue, you would still have to do more personal work on it after the clearing is done. Yes, if you do use that untapped issue for Ancestral Lines Clearing, your subsequent work would last. The problem would not circle back around again, unless there is another facet of it to be worked on.

However, for at least your first experience with the process, choose an issue you have already worked on. Experience first-hand the benefits of this process and there will be more likelihood that you will want to use it again. You do not have to do all of the work in one experience. It is much easier and more satisfying to take it in bits and pieces.

In Chapter One you read about my first experience. That was done with the topic of a "mere" attitude that I had worked on in depth and thought I had cleared. The Ancestral Lines

Clearing progressed quickly, only fifteen minutes start to finish, and I was inspired to do further clearings later on as needed. Several years later I tackled a much larger issue, as it turned out. That one took over an hour for one side of the family to be cleared. I took a break and then later came back to clear the other family lines for close to an hour more. It was excruciating! If I had done that particular issue the first time, I would never have continued the process, much less teach it and write about it!

Remember: This book is telling you exactly how to do the clearing work. You do not have to get everything done in one session alone. You can come back and do another session on a different facet of the same issue as before. It is better to enjoy and feel release after each short session than to plod through one huge difficult one.

Aspect of Your Issue

It may be surprising that what you think is the issue to use for your Ancestral Lines Clearing may not be what Spirit knows you are to use.

For example, in the late 1990's one of my students, "Gina", knew she would be working on the abuse she had suffered as a child. She had done a lot of counseling, healing and even soul retrievals over the years and yet, aspects of it continued to plague her. When she journeyed to ask her High Self what aspect of the abuse issue she was to use for our workshop, she did so with a firm knowing that she wanted the truth. Her High Self told her to use a specific attitude. She had expected a bigger chunk of the issue than that, but accepted its wisdom. With the Ho'oponopono Ritual, she felt waves of release. Upon clearing her father's family lines, tears of relief streamed down her face. At the end of clearing her mother's family lines, she exuded joy in the sheer knowing that a deep healing had occurred. At the same time, she was astonished at how clearing a "mere attitude" could produce such profound effects within her.

Obtaining clarity on which aspect of your issue is to be used is crucial for healing you and your family lines. As an analogy, think of a plate of food at dinner. You do not pour the whole contents into your mouth all at the same time. You choose where to start, and just enjoy this delicious way of replenishing your energy. Just so, the Ancestral Lines Clearing process does not deal with an entire issue all at once. Such problems as alcoholism, abuse, lack of abundance, low self esteem, to name only a few, have many complicated components to them. Metaphorically, they could be considered a smorgasbord instead of just a plate of food.

The choice of component is best left up to the wisdom of your High Self, i.e., the highest wisdom possible. If you choose it with your left-brain thinking, there is the chance of thinking it is a simple facet only to find out it is a huge "iceberg." You may end up biting off more than you can chew, so to speak. The High Self understands and knows what is most appropriate for your healing at the moment.

One client in private session chose what she said her High Self told her to use for her first Ancestral Lines Clearing. During the clearing of each ancestral lines, it seemed to me that she was falling asleep. I asked her what was going on. She said she was going into trance so deeply that she could not remember much about it. She, rather than her High Self, had chosen the issue for the Ancestral Lines Clearing. It was too big a chunk to deal with at one time. She could not keep proper focus.

Modalities For Clearing

Spirit will do all of the work of clearing your ancestral lines. It knows where and in whom the problems are located, in each generation. That alone is a mammoth task! Spirit also has access to each person's High Self in order to obtain permission for the clearing. Your High Self has access to the highest energies of highest Spirit that are needed in order to clear the entire ancestral lines of this particular aspect of the issue. It also knows how precise the energy has to work at times in order to excise only the exact strands of energy symbolized by the aspect of the trait you are working on. No human can do that work. We can watch it being done and can imagine we are doing exactly what we saw Spirit doing. But we do not carry the power nor the ability to achieve the clearing. Only your High Self and spirit guides of that high level are the ones who can.

What Spirit does require of you is to keep the focus. Ability to keep continual focus on what is transpiring helps you to know when to step in with the Ho'oponopono Rite when it is needed. Ability to keep continual focus on what is transpiring also gives Spirit permission to do this work. In that way, you are turning your free will over to Spirit. Ability to keep continual focus on what is transpiring allows you to be the proxy for your entire ancestral lines in removing that component of the DNA. You are doing this work initially for yourself, and secondarily for members of your ancestral lines. What a beautiful gift you are giving yourself and them!

In order to keep the focus, you need to know several things: what configuration the ancestral lines are in, the high-powered element your High Self will use for clearing, and how to follow the ebb and flow of that energy. Your High Self will give you that information. In order to keep your ego from skewing the information, it is imperative that you be totally focused on wanting the truth whether it fits with your desires or not. If you choose the element or symbols, you could well be sabotaging the whole process. The High Self has great wisdom and will choose wisely for you. Trust that.

Form of Trance to Use

This process is more easily done within a shamanic journey than in any other trance style. Still, it is possible to do it in other forms of trance, such as self-hypnosis or guided imagery, if you have a strong connection with your High Self or spirit guide. If you cannot do any of that, do not worry. You can enlist an energy worker to do the clearing for you.

Components of the Clearing Process

Spiritual power element. All Spiritual power is vibration. In your mind's perception it tends to show up in some form of the "four elements" of fire, water, air and earth. The key here is to ask for the highest most powerful form of whatever element or combination of elements the High Self knows it will use to clear your family lines. For instance, if the element is light, the clearing goes faster with a laser-beam than with a flashlight.

Symbol of your family's lines. One of the ways to help you keep focused on what your High Self is clearing, is to know the way your High Self views your ancestral lines. In trance, you will ask your High Self to show you what the symbol is for your ancestry. Whether it is an earthen path, a fleur de lys, a cross, maze, Medicine Wheel, river, combination of different images or some other symbol, accept it. There is no template for what a pattern should be. Configurations are strictly up to the High Self, who knows what symbology best fits you.

Then you will ask it how you are to follow its clearing-energy through that symbol, how you will notice when the energy is stalled so that you can do the Ho'oponopono Rite to clear the block, and how to know when the clearing is complete. Your High Self's answers may be quite unique. They may help you keep your focus from wandering, as well as to know more clearly any minute details that bring deeper understanding to your issue and your life.

Chapter Seven

Full Walk Through

Modalities Preparation

This book describes how to do the clearing work. You do not have to get everything done in one session alone. You can always do another Ancestral Lines Clearing on other aspects of the issue, later. In each case, gather information when you are on a shamanic journey or in trance. For simplicity's sake I am referring only to journeying and the High Self from here on; if you choose to do a different form of trance or use a Spirit Guide instead, merely translate to that as you read.

At first it is best to do a separate journey for each facet italicized below. Ask your High Self only one question at a time and get clarification as needed. That way, there will be no confusion about what part of your dialogue is being answered. One question at a time greatly clarifies everything in your mind. Trust Spirit and want the truth regardless if it is the same or different from what you would like or expect.

The following three preparation components are in the order that is most efficient and beneficial for the process.

Facet of the Issue. Here are the steps for enlisting the aid of your High Self in choosing the issue and its facet for the Ancestral Lines Clearing.

1. Enter the shamanic journey.

2. Call in your High Self. Be sure you sincerely want the truth from your High Self.

3. Present to your High Self several issues that you have already worked to heal. If you have not worked on given issues, delete them from your list.

4. Ask your High Self which issue would achieve the most effective results for an Ancestral Lines Clearing at this time. Ask follow-up questions for clarity.

5. Ask it what facet of the issue would give you the most effective results at this time. Ask follow-up questions for clarity and detail regarding the answer.

6. Resolve to adhere to the wisdom of your High Self.

7. Decide which side of your family seems to have the most "charge," i.e., bring up the most negative emotions, in causing the problem: your father's or your mother's or your adoptive parents (if that applies to your situation)? The side that resonates the most with the issue-facet is the side of the family to start with for the Ancestral Lines Clearing.

8. Return from the journey and write down whatever notes and details your High Self gave you.

Spiritual Element for Clearing. Ask your High Self what high-powered spiritual element it will use for the clearing of this family line. Remember: for effective results it must be your High Self who chooses the element it will use.

Symbol of this side of your family lines. Gather the following information from your High Self. Discuss as needed. When each answer is clear to you, proceed to the next one.

1. What is the symbol for this branch of your ancestral lines?

2. How am I to follow its clearing progress with the high-powered energy?

3. How am I to know when the energy stalls or is blocked, so that I can do the Ho'oponopono Rite?

4. How am I to know when the clearing is finished?

Ho'oponopono Ritual

You are now ready to start the Ancestral Lines Clearing. The first part of the work involves the Ho'oponopono Ritual for the parent whose background tells you that this side of your ancestry is the more significant one in causing your DNA-distorted issue. There are two segments to the ritual:

• forgiving all members of that side of your family: everyone you have ever known or heard about or read about, including preceding generations, your siblings, cousins, children, and all living members of subsequent generations. This is to be done in a group format, initially; to do the ritual for each person alone would take you days!

• accepting forgiveness from them, also in group format initially. Obviously, you are doing this without being in their presence. Spirit is in charge here and is proxy for your family accepting the forgiveness. Each person will be assisted by their High Self. Hawaiians explain why this is effective by saying that all High Selves of an ancestry form a council of High Selves called the Poe Aumakua. They are always in communication with each other and can convey messages and healing directions accordingly. In other words, group format is highly effective.

Family members will leave the scene spontaneously when their High Self knows the process is complete for them. You may find that a few stay in the scene. Do the rite again, for all that stay. When the crowd dwindles to individuals, you may intuitively know whether to do the rite in a small group format, or individually. Trust what you feel in this matter. Continue until all leave the scene, or your High Self says it is OK for them to stay.

The Ho'oponopono Ritual Itself. At the end of each of the steps below, take a few moments to feel it within your entire being. Let this be an energetic "knowing" sense within you. When you are ready to progress to the next step, do so.

1. Ask your High Self to completely fill you with and surround you by its brightest, purest, spiritual light possible. Rest in the light and energy a few minutes before continuing.

2. Picture at a comfortable distance from you, everyone you ever knew or heard of on this side of the family. Let them be surrounded by the light of their own choosing. Do not tamper with their light.

3. Notice the connection between you and all of them.

4. Say and experience the Ho'oponopono rite as given in italics below. When you see the three dots within the script, pause and experience deep sincerity and release of those negative family ties. Know that the positive/constructive ties will always remain.

> **Inwardly say to this side of your family, _as a_**
> **_group_ and as sincerely as possible:**
> _"I forgive all of you for all the hurts that you have done_
> _to me regarding this issue (state the issue),..._
> _both real and imagined,... known and unknown,..._
> _intentional and unintentional,..._
> _from the beginning of time to the present..._
> _And I release you from all of these..."_

Let your ties to them drop away from you. Do nothing to the ties your family members carry. Enlist the help of your High Self if you have difficulty letting your ties go. Allow the release to continue until all ties fall off that are going to. Then go onto the following.

> **Inwardly say to your family, _as a group_ and**
> **as sincerely as possible:**
> _"I accept your forgiveness of me for all the hurts that I_
> _have done to you regarding this same issue,..._
> _both real and imagined,... known and unknown,..._
> _intentional and unintentional,..._
> _from the beginning of time to the present..._
> _And I accept your release of me from all of these..."_

Let your ties to them drop away from you. Do nothing to the ties your family members carry. Enlist the help of your High Self if you have difficulty letting your ties go. Allow the release to continue until all ties fall off that are going to. If not all ties fall off, repeat both parts of the Ho'oponopono.

5. If the forgiveness ritual stalls, check your sincerity to let go of the cords and energy. When you know you have done your part fully, then ask your High Self what needs to happen to complete the process. If it is still not clear, discuss the situation with your High Self. When the answer is plausible, the situation should resolve itself.

6. Ask your High Self to fill your vacated spaces with its bright spiritual light and reinforcement.

7. Occasionally a family member will stay behind because he or she wants to watch your clearing process. Consult

your High Self and your own instinct regarding whether this is alright or not.

Working with Your High Self

Your High Self is in charge of the actual clearing of your family lines. Your responsibilities are to keep focused on what is happening and to do the Ho'oponopono as needed. Here is the detailed instruction.

1. After linking to your High Self, direct it to clear that side of your family lines from now through all time to when the problem originated. If any variation in that now-to-the-past direction shows up spontaneously and you know you did not stipulate it, let your High Self continue in the manner it is directing you. (See the "Variations In The Process" chapter for clarification of this.) However, if you had decided that the directions should be different, immediately let go of your presumption and let the High Self do the work as it deems best. You will understand why, later.

2. Your role in the process is to keep focused on the symbol of your family lines and follow the energy source your High Self is using to clear the lines.

3. What to do if the energy stalls? Here is a non-prioritized list of possible symptoms that there a block in the path that caused the energy to stall:

> you feel fatigued
> you doze off
> your mind wanders constantly
> an image of a specific culture and time appears
> you think "this is just not getting anywhere"
> the family symbol shows that the energy has stopped

4. At that signal, do the Ho'oponopono Rite to clear the block. Your High Self may or may not give you images or information about the block. Even if you do not know why it is needed, still do both sides of the Ho'oponopono until the High Self resumes its clearing energy again. Trust its wisdom.

5. When the block is removed, the High Self will resume its process again. On the other hand, if you know the block has been removed yet the High Self has not resumed its

clearing, it probably is because the issue you are clearing is part of your karma. That means you have to give Spirit the "OK" to continue the clearing. By doing this, you indicate to Spirit that you have progressed in your learning. Bravo/ Brava!

6. If a block will not clear, ask your High Self what needs to happen. If your High Self does not respond, it probably is telling you that you already know what to do. However, just in case it is needed, here are some suggestions. They are not in any particular order.

• As you speak the Rite, be truthful and sincere that you are releasing any hurt you have felt regarding the issue.

• If an ancestor or current family member seems to be hanging onto your energy, speak the rite and call your High Self to take that person's energy from you.

• Ask your High Self to call in any of your family members' High Selves that are able and willing to help you with the work.

• Refer to any instructions previously given you by your High Self.

7. Whichever of the above ways works, resume the clearing when the High Self gives the "go ahead" for it.

8. If there are more blocks along the way, do the rite each time.

9. The clearing continues until your High Self shows you, by way of instruction through the family symbol or otherwise, that the work is finished. You might also experience a sense of relief or lightness in energy.

Subsequent Sides of Your Ancestral Lines

The process for clearing the other sides of your ancestral lines follows the same general pattern you used for the "first side."

You must use the very same issue and facet you used for the first side of your ancestral lines!

That is because this parent played into or abetted the actions of the parent who was causal in the issue. In the process of clearing, insights will spring up to help you realize how significant this side of the family was in creating or maintaining the dysfunction. This side may be quicker to clear than the first side. On the other hand, it may be surprisingly more complicated and difficult.

1. Follow all of the above steps for this side of the family just like you did for the "causal" side. Do not skip any component, other than the issue-facet being used for the exercise. The energy element and symbol sometimes are similar but often are quite different.

2. When the clearing for all family sides is completed, continue on with the rest of the steps below.

Clearing Your Future

Clearing your future is necessary because of a great gift Spirit has given you over the years. Meaning, that on various occasions there inevitably may have been an overload of ancestral issues about to descend upon you. Your soul would have been overwhelmed or so heavily burdened by it that it would have been detrimental to you and your spiritual growth. Spirit's gift was to shunt ancestral issues to a future time when you could better deal with it. Right now is one of those better times, and Spirit will help you clear it with little to no stress on you. Here is your future-clearing pattern:

1. Ask your High Self what high-powered element it will use to clear your future.

2. Ask your High Self for the symbol of your own future.

3. Ask how to follow the energy element's clearing through that symbol.

4. This stage does not require the Ho'oponopono at the beginning. You completed that when you did the parental Ancestral Lines Clearings.

5. Start right out by directing your High Self to clear your future.

6. If the clearing stalls, do the Ho'oponopono to that spot.

7. Direct the High Self to resume clearing when the block is removed.

8. When the future is cleared, ask your High Self to replenish your energy. Rest in that awareness for a few minutes.

"Doorstep"

Over the years of metaphysical work I have often heard it said that as we do our own work, we help the rest of the world heal. I always thought that meant changing the energy around me, making it easier for others to feel comfortable in my presence and perhaps also in their own skin. Probably this is true. However, when my spirit teacher told me to bring the healing of my first Ancestral Lines Clearing up to the doorstep of my family members, the "helping the rest of the world to heal" evoked deep gratitude and awe in the magnitude of Spirit's work. Over the years this evolved into delight at seeing how far around the world the healing was extending. And indeed, often I can see the light of healing extend around the globe many times, or little lights popping up in various parts of the world as a result of the "doorstep" facet.

The "doorstep" pattern:

1. In this final stage, ask your High Self to take the healing up to the doorstep of every living family member, whether known or unknown. This lets each family member accept the healing if, or when, they choose it.

2. Let images come to mind but do not command that specific people appear. Your High Self will give you only those faces and general images it knows are pertinent to your awareness.

3. If the High Self refuses to put the healing on the doorstep of a particular person, honor that action. The person would probably misuse the gift, to their own detriment.

Chapter Eight

Variations in the Process

Configurations

Over the years my Spirit Teacher had me clear the lines in different ways. At first everything started in the present and cleared back through the ages to the beginning of the issue at hand. Later he had me start way back in the past, healing where the problem began then clearing the lines up to the present. Another time he felt it would be easier and more effective to alternate between part of Mom's line then part of Dad's, over and over until both lines were cleared. And one time he had me clear my personal future before even starting on clearing the ancestral lines past.

My Dad's line has always followed the same path as in the initial channeling. My Mom's line, though, changes according to the issue. Much of the time her clearing goes east first and then heads south. Sometimes it has gone up in the air to traverse the directions and sometimes down onto the "earth" and sometimes it has gone in a spiral diagonally. These variations may be mystifying, but they do get the job done.

The ease – or lack of it – in clearing the lines varies a lot. My students and clients usually find that the first side takes longer or feels more difficult than the other. Initially I thought that was because the issue chosen was so prevalent within that family line. Then there were times it was surprisingly the opposite; the second side was more difficult to clear than the first. Such occurrences are very insightful, revealing hidden agendas on both sides of the family.

There were also a few times that the actual onset of the issue was not the problem at all. In reality, the onset was quite innocent or even magnanimous and spiritual. Then, generations later, a dramatic event such as "taking a virtue to a fault" occurred that anchored the dysfunctional attitude into the DNA. This happened with one particular facet of my own family lines clearing.

The issue I used for the Ancestral Lines Clearing was lack-of-abundance. The pivotal point was in the Middle Ages at a monastery that vowed poverty. Try as I would, no amount of Ho'oponopono could release the event enough to get my High Self's energy started again. My High Self then had me call for the High Selves of any Horn family members who were willing to help clear that highly pivotal point. Instantly, those of my father (still alive) and two of his Lutheran-ministerial brothers (deceased) came in. With all of that high-powered light working in tandem, the knots and twists and myriad convolutions were finally sorted out and transmuted. Instantly, my relatives and their High Selves disappeared and the way opened up for my High Self to continue alone on the path of clearing. When we reached the beginning of the issue, I saw that what started the dysfunction was a generous action with caring intent; it was quite noble and spiritual. Standing by itself, it would not have altered our family's DNA into a dysfunctional trait. Whatever happened in the Middle Ages turned that virtue into a hindrance.

The differences in procedure are dictated by Spirit according to what is the most expedient way to clear a specific issue-facet from the ancestral lines. Any details that show up are ones that Spirit knows we need for our healing.

Other Variations

Past-Life Influences at times show up while clearing the lines. Here are two illustrations of variations I have witnessed:

• *After taking the Ancestral Lines Clearing workshop, a friend remarked that all of her past-lives had been in the same ancestral lineage as her current family!*

• *In several instances of my own clearings I was shown that a few of my current relatives had also incarnated in our lineage hundreds of years ago. At the appropriate generation, only their faces showed up; there was no energy indicating a soul part stuck in the past. That was Spirit's way of helping me understand how formative that person's presence has been in our lineage.*

Deceased Relative Helps

In 2010 I did a clearing of another issue that began with my father's family lines. When my High Self got to the late 1700s, it pulled me into that scene. Unexpectedly, my deceased father flew in! He looked exactly as he did at the age of 85, sparse white hair and all, although with a lot more vibrant energy. He and his High Self had been given Spirit's sanction to help me clear that segment of the issue because he had been working on it in spirit, between lives! When we finished that segment, he suddenly transformed into the red-haired energetic self that he was at 38 years old. Both he and his High Self disappeared from the scene. My High Self told me the rest was up to us.

Soul Retrieval

In shamanic soul retrievals there are occasional instances that a soul part is brought back from a past life. However, not all of the person's past-life soul parts are returned in one soul retrieval. The same is true of Ancestral Lines Clearing. It is up to Spirit to determine the appropriateness of such a retrieval. Here are some that I have witnessed.

• *A private-session client saw herself as a Native American during an Ancestral Lines Clearing. As that self, she had married into the family that is now her current lineage. She also saw that a piece of her had stayed in that past-life, meaning, it did not go on to Spirit realms when she died. So we brought that piece forward into her now. This was a case of spontaneous soul retrieval for her; she was ready for it.*

• *In one instance my spirit teacher showed me that my aunt had been in my grandfather's lineage in the early 1800s and had left a piece of her soul there. He plucked her soul part out and sent it off to her current life self! I asked him why he did not send it up to her High Self, as he usually did when someone is still alive? (Thinking: Why are we doing the "no no" of an un-asked-for healing?) He said that she had less than a year left in this life. She needed her soul parts back within her so that she could make a clean transition to the Light when she died.*

"Doorstep."

In a client's private session I witnessed the Archangels spontaneously doing an Ancestral Lines Clearing during the energy work. When they got to the "doorstep" segment, one person they offered it to is not my client's relative in this life time. When I asked the Archangels about it, they said that he was offered the healing because he was part of the family lineage in a previous lifetime. Apparently he was ready for a past-life healing as part of his present spiritual growth.

Energy Healing

In most energy healing sessions, the Archangels use a high powered light much like a white laser beam to transmute a past-life or ancestral-line. They often do this when my client does not need to know the details. Chances are, the person has already healed the underlying issues and merely needs the past cleared so that it does not influence the present. In several cases, though, the Archangels have done massive clearing of an ancestral line. At the same time they shared pertinent details that gave my client deeper insight into how the ancestral lineage has affected him or her in this life.

One of my shamanism students gave me the following account of an energetic healing she did that included Ancestral Lines Clearing. Here is her account.

"My daughter, Bobbi, was diagnosed with a large ovarian tumor. At the time, medical experts did not know whether it was cancerous, but they scheduled surgery within ten days due to the medical history of our family: aunt dying of ovarian cancer, grandfather dying of colon cancer, grandmother dying of breast cancer, and a cousin who had frequent and numerous benign ovarian tumors. It seemed that an Ancestral Lines Clearing was definitely in order.

"After shamanically connecting into my healing team, Archangels Azrael, Gabriel, and Sandalphon, I asked them to

remove the causative spiritual-energy-agent for the tumor's growth. That they did.

"Then I asked Archangel Azrael to clear Bobbi's ancestral lines. When he stretched forth his right hand, beams of cleansing energy spread from her solar plexus outward to include her ancestral lines. Being a relative, I got instant confirmation, with an exhilarating feeling radiating within my Solar Plexus. Next Azrael proceeded to clear her future lives and I saw a sonic-like energy pulsing behind her. He indicated that this was where the healing was needed. Again I felt an immediate response. As her current life was cleared, a beam shot from her crown chakra down through her root chakra and she was bathed in gentle rotating rays. Finally, her past lives were cleared and energy poured into the root chakra. The color changed from dull red darkness to a bright clear red. In response to her lives being cleared, I felt a washing of energy down my legs and out the soles of my feet.

"After the Ancestral Lines Clearing, Archangel Azrael stated, 'She will be troubled by this no more.' Through the physical confirmations I received during Bobbi's healing, I had absolutely no doubt of the truth of his promise.

"Bobbi's surgery was performed; the tumor was benign. It is a comfort to have the truth that she, her daughters, and future generations will not be plagued by a problem that has persisted for so many lifetimes."

Ancestral lines healing, not clearing. As is true with a lot of channeled work, there will inevitably be variations that occur according to individual need. Please understand that the variations are given by Spirit, not by our individual wills. That is true when you do your own Ancestral Lines Clearing and true when an energy worker does the work for you. The right configuration of healing will occur if you both are sincere in wanting the truth regardless of how it comes about, known or unknown, convenient or uncomfortable.

One such variation occurred in early 2012. I was doing energy work for a client, who I call "Sarah," when Archangel Raphael stepped in and said that we needed to do ancestral lines healing, instead of clearing. He stipulated that the family lines exhibited little love, not because there were blocks to love, but because significant amounts of love were missing.

Kind of like a person suffering "soul loss," this in a sense was a case of the lines missing the spiritual trait of love.

"Sarah's" Healing. On the day that we were to do this Ancestral Lines Healing, Archangel Raphael moved to the front, i.e., more recent, of Sarah's ancestral lines. Gently and quietly he inserted a wee bit of love at the head of the lines. Then he stood back and watched. He said he was waiting to see how the current family reacted to the amount of love he had inserted. It was important that the amount put in would not overwhelm them. If they were to feel overwhelmed, they could react adversely and actually eject what was put in. That act of inadvertent sabotage would continue, making it harder to insert more love later.

It felt like we were waiting a very long time, so I spoke to tell Sarah briefly what we were doing, and that I would explain why, later. (For those of you who are unfamiliar with shamanic journeying, it is important to tell you of the peculiarities in sensing the length of time while on a journey. Long story short, what may feel like a half hour may only be about five minutes in clock time. And what may feel like only a couple of minutes may actually be a half hour. This peculiarity is very common in journeying but can also be experienced in any life endeavor in which you are so engrossed in what is happening that you lose all track of time.)

After this very long time (maybe five minutes?), Archangel Raphael inserted more love even deeper at another point a bit farther back in the lines. Again we waited for what seemed a very long time. Then he said, "This is enough for today. We will check in on the lines every couple of days for a week or more, to see how the current-day family is handling it."

That we did. Finally, though, it was over a month before he said it was time to insert more love. This time he went back further in time to another generation and inserted love deeper still. Again we waited a long time. When he noticed that the family lines accepted the love, he went to an even more distant generation. This time he inserted love extremely deep, to what looked like the "spine" of the family lines. He then closed up the aura of the lines and he and I moved back to the inner platform I clairvoyantly see when I do shamanic healing and aura cleansing.

Interestingly, Sarah said her mother called her that evening "for no reason, just wanted to talk." That motive was uncharacteristic of her. Her voice carried more gentleness and love in it than usual. Obviously, Archangel Raphael's "love retrieval" for the family lines was highly effective

Chapter Nine

Personal Follow-ups

The Ancestral Lines Clearing process clears from your ancestral DNA the unhealthy facet of the issue needing healing. It does not clear unfinished business with your own karma regarding the issue. For that, you may need to continue working on it. The blessing of all of this is that once you have fully cleared the issue and learned the lesson, it will not recycle as it did before.

There are two adjuncts to the Ancestral Lines Clearing that may immediately resolve your own issues so that there need be no further effort. One is to remove any family soul parts that may be embedded within your aura. The other is to locate dysfunctional beliefs directly relating to the facet cleared, and change those beliefs to functional ones. If you were to leave the residue in your being, it could still control you to the extent of causing you to slip back into the old issue. It is a strong control. Yet it is fairly simple to remove the soul parts, discover dysfunctional beliefs and change them to functional ones.

Other people's soul parts need to be removed first so that they do not tell you their beliefs rather than you accurately discovering your own.

Soul Part Removal

Chances are, the Ho'oponopono Rite will have sent off many soul parts from other family members. Nevertheless, this process needs to at least be looked into to make sure you are totally cleared of them. The reason this is important is because any one else's soul part on you interferes with who you truly are, the values you have, the way you think and the way you feel. This may sound strange, but your soul has a unique vibration, as does everyone else's. Each vibration is meant to be autonomous. It is not meant to intermix with other vibrations. Essentially, another person's soul part affects you negatively and can cause others to view you negatively. The same energy on the soul to whom it belongs, shows up as light, uplifting energy.

When others' soul parts are removed from you, you may feel a more uplifted energy and mood. It is like releasing a twenty-five-pound load from your shoulders. Such a relief! It frees you up for more creative and uplifting endeavors. You may also glean beneficial insights concerning how you were affected by the soul parts being on you. To further illustrate this, here is one client's experience:

"Grace" found that with each soul part she identified and released came a realization of why she had experienced consistent negative attitudes and abilities in her life. The dysfunctional feeling of self doubt came from her father's rejection of her penchant for going inward to contact Spirit and wanting to express herself through creativity. He exerted rigid control of every facet of her life including how she was to be and to come across to others. She could not be herself. As she released her father's soul parts to her spirit helpers to take to his High Self, she excitedly regained more self-composure and truth of who she really is.

Her self loathing came from her mother's constant critical nit-picking and yelling at her, not only throughout her life, but also from her mother's soul part inside her head, 24/7. No matter what she did or said to herself, she could never please her mother. She felt like a failure even though she won sports awards as a young girl and achieved success in her career. When her power animals took her mother's soul parts away, her mood started to lift at once. The negative feelings gave way to true attitudes of loving herself more and believing in herself more.

Her self hatred came from her twin sister's jealousy of her and casting jealous soul parts onto her. Over the years that the soul parts were on her, she kept trying to change the situation outwardly with her sister "Reya." Nothing got solved in the relationship by trying this. However, letting her spirit helpers take away Reya's soul parts brought in tremendous relief. She no longer had to "own" those feelings of self-hate. She knew it was Reya's problem, not hers.

She also discovered why she had trouble with boundaries and her relationship with her husband. The boundaries problem came from her mother's soul parts making her feel guilty if she did not allow enmeshment in their relationship. Also, part of the difficult relationship with her husband came from her father's soul parts constantly exuding disharmony within her mind and feelings. This kept her from being her true self. By discovering and releasing her parents' soul parts, she knew her marital relationship would immediately improve. What a wonderful relief!

Grace's had already done considerable inner healing work prior to this experience. She found it enlivening to release these many soul parts. That, and the instantaneous realizations that came with them, took perhaps ten minutes after the Ancestral Lines Clearing was completed.

Releasing others' soul parts is not done through the Ho'oponopono Rite. That is because forgiveness is a process of releasing bonds that tie you unnaturally to other people. In removing others' soul parts, however, you release soul energy. Holding those soul parts within your aura is what psychologists metaphorically call "carrying other people's baggage," meaning, attitudes and habits taken on from significant others in your life. Shamanically, we know that it is no metaphor; it is actual energy that was taken on. Not only that, but intelligent energy. This intelligent energy of someone else's soul part talks into your mind 24/7. Think of a family member being around you all the time, constantly giving you their opinion and not caring to hear yours. In physical life that probably would cause irritations, confusion and turbulence in your relationship. If persistent, it could also interfere with your values, your thoughts and your true way of being. It is the same way with another's soul part in your mind and aura, as the following client accounts show.

"Joan's" Story. Joan was so emotionally intent on helping her son stand up for himself that she inadvertently gave part of her soul to him. Instead of helping him, she created the opposite affect. The soul part hindered him from learning how to be self-supporting. He felt resentful and became even more powerless to act on his own behalf. At the same time, she felt an energy drain from her soul part leaving, as well as growing ineptness in her ability to help. Hard feelings built up between the two.

"Rosalee's" Story. During a soul transformation session, Rosalee did a shamanic journey to her twelve-year-old soul part. It brought to her awareness the memory of an inner incident which Rosalee did not recall ever having in physical life nor prior to the soul retrieval. In the memory, she was standing motionless in her school's hallway, while her friend "Milly" shouted at her constantly. Milly told her she was "bad, a no-good worthless person and would rot in hell for what she did!" At the same time, Rosalee contradicted this by saying to herself current day truths such as, "I am creatively talented, a top scholar, and am successful in my work. I have close friends and have always been spiritually motivated."

After Rosalee and I worked with this self-belief she noticed a difference in the hall scene. She saw three images of her friend all at the same time! I realized that Milly had angrily flung several of her soul parts at Rosalee. These soul parts were a major cause of Rosalee's low opinion of herself. Every time she thought well of herself, Milly's soul parts contradicted her. It was a continual battle every hour of every day, and had been for decades.

How did the soul parts get there, to begin with? It is called "soul stealing" if you took them and "soul giving or soul flinging" if someone else sent them to you. Giving and stealing soul parts is a common occurrence in society. Unfortunately, it always leads to strife between the two of you, and with both of you feeling less able to cope with the relationship. Others' soul parts do not help us. Carrying others' soul parts causes inner conflict and increased friction in relationships. The inner conflict produces more negativity: increased anger, strife, control, reprisal, being out of control, inciting problems with loved ones, loss of soul parts, loss of energy, loss of sleep, lack of peace. If you think and act hatefully toward the person who owns the soul parts you are carrying, you may become abusive or allow yourself to be abused. This, in turn, increases a sense of guilt, fear and/or low self-worth. It is a cycle that forever spirals downward. There is no benefit to keeping their soul energy.

Symptoms of Others' Soul Parts on You
• You over react to the other person's actions or words.
• The other person "pushes your buttons" easily.
• You daydream about arguing with that person.
• You feel an inner contradiction to your values, beliefs.
• You feel inner contradiction to wanting to take action.
• You feel anxiety when others' soul parts first come to you. It is because you have more energy than you know what to do with. It may also feel like that person is right next to you.

Symptoms of Soul Stealing in Progress
• After intense emotional expression with someone, you feel an energy drain that gets worse as time goes on.
• You suddenly become very sleepy or groggy, whereas moments ago you were alert.
• You feel drained of energy when near the person.
• You feel drained of energy when you think of them.
• The energy drain is a big signal that the stealing may be going on right now.

Removing Others' Soul Parts
High Self work. After having read the above "Symptoms" sections you may find yourself more cognizant of family members speaking in your mind. Strange as that may sound, it really is how others' soul parts may act. There could be thoughts you recognize as coming from a specific person. You may see images of the person in your mind. You may feel negative emotions towards specific relatives each time you think of them. Each of these is a symptom of part of that person's soul stuck in your aura. To release them, there needs

71

to be powerful intelligent spiritual energy involved. If you worked effectively with the High Self during the Ancestral Lines Clearing, then it is that powerful being who can remove the soul parts for you. If you can do shamanic journeying, your power animals con remove them.

You must also be fully willing to "let go and let God" in your awareness. To do this, call in your High Self to fill you and surround you with its light. Proceed with the Ho'oponopono Ritual for each person who comes to mind. Do this only one person at a time. The fact that a person's soul part is still entrenched in your being indicates that it needs one-on-one in-depth attention. Continue to enlist the help of your High Self to take the soul part away. Be sincere in your willingness to let go of the person and release any hard feelings you have toward them.

If the Ho'oponopono Ritual has no effect, and you do not know how to do shamanic journeying, it would be advisable to consult a professional energy worker to do it for you.

Trance work. Soul part removal usually is most accurately done during a shamanic journey or with an energy worker removing them for you. Here is another way of doing this:

1. On a shamanic journey, preferably to the lower world, contact the power animal who you most trust.

2. Ask that being to identify anyone else's soul parts within you or your aura.

3. When it does that, ask it to take that soul part off to its own High Self. It must not go back directly to the person it belongs to, because that action would be an unrequested healing. The person may not be ready for it and s/he could just send them back to you. Sending it to the person's High Self allows that great being to determine when is the right timing to return it safely.

4. When the power animal returns, ask it to find any other soul parts of your family and take them to their High Selves as well. Continue doing this until your power animal tells you there are no more soul parts on you.

Changing Beliefs

Our beliefs govern our attitudes, thoughts and actions. For example: There is a commonly held attitude in society of "I'll believe it when I see it." In truth, we often do not see it until we *believe* it. Meaning, a paradigm shift has to happen before we will see or understand a different point of view. The attitude or belief may start in childhood, taking on the beliefs and attitudes of our parents or other primary caregivers. If those people leave parts of their soul on us, those soul parts keep reinforcing their beliefs and attitudes in our mind. This is the crucial reason why soul parts have to be removed before we can effectively work with identifying and changing beliefs.

"R.L.'s Story. As part of clearing her ancestral lines of an addiction impulse, Archangel Michael removed detrimental energies, discarnates and fear that kept pushing her to smoke another cigarette. It was the proverbial "War in the Heavens" from past lives up to the present. He cleared the power grid of the whole planet of detrimental forces, including a deception "cloud" that keeps a person from knowing the truth of what is going on. This deception relates to the addictive impulse in general. How it shows up in someone is a personal tendency or preference.

During her follow-up work she uncovered a dysfunctional belief that "there is always something more," meaning that what she has now is not enough. Her spirit guides helped her to realize that the true belief is "God's love and light are here, and that is always enough."

After others' soul parts have been sent off, you can more easily identify your own dysfunctional beliefs and discard any that had been constantly spoken into your mind by other people's soul parts. Here is a pattern you can use on a shamanic journey in conjunction with your spirit helper or High Self:

1. Have your spirit helper peruse your beliefs, and inform you of any dysfunctional belief you have regarding the issue that has just been cleared from your DNA.

2. Dialogue with that spirit helper until you have a complete grasp on what the belief is about and how it has affected your thoughts, emotions and behavior.

3. Ask the spirit helper to remove the power from that belief. Notice how the energy changes and how your attitude changes as well.

> If you leave the process right there, you create a vacuum.
> Nature abhors a vacuum.
> There needs to be a replacement belief put in,
> so that the old one does not return.

4. Ask your spirit helper to tell you the replacement belief.

5. Dialogue with that spirit helper until you have a complete grasp on what the belief is about and how it feels at every level within you. If it does not feel true enough, it will feel like the old belief is starting to return. In that case, ask your spirit helper to go deeper and find the true belief that will definitely replace the old one.

6. Continue the dialogue with your spirit helper until you know that any deeper belief will adequately replace the dysfunctional belief.

7. Ask your spirit helper to put power into it. Notice how the energy changes and how your attitude changes as well.

8. At this point, retrace your steps from the journey and return to ordinary life awareness.

Homework.

Over the next several weeks, be aware of your beliefs and endeavor to use them in your life. There may be times when you feel, think or behave spontaneously in the new way; when you realize that, thank yourself and Spirit. There may be times when your inner mind gives you the choice: go with the new way or go back to the old pattern? Then choose the new way; thank yourself, your inner mind and Spirit. If there are any times that you think, feel or act in the old way and you suddenly realize that after the fact, vow that the next time you will choose the new way. Then thank yourself, your inner mind and Spirit.

I am not exactly sure why any of the three realizations occurs. What is important, though, is that you realize it, that you vow to go with the new, and that you thank Spirit and all aspects of yourself. Doing this reinforces not only the recent changes, but also boosts your self-esteem.

Also over the next several weeks, keep a log of anything new. You may notice a difference in your feelings, your outlook on life, your attitude towards others and life, your attitude towards the world, how you view nature. Others may comment on a difference in you, or may be different in their interaction with you. If anyone remarks about how different you look or act, say "thank you!"....to them out loud, and to yourself and Spirit within.

Do not discount anything new! Do not say to yourself, "oh yes, that's new, but I've already been working on that for years." Instead, say, "oh yes, that's new. I've worked on it for years. Yeay! Yet it also relates to the Ancestral Lines Clearing and the beliefs and soul parts work. Yeay! I needed all of that for this change to finally click in." After about a week of keeping meticulous records of new things, read through your log. It is then that you will be able to discern what is new because of this work, what is new solely due to other inner work, and what is new just because you are looking for something new. From this self-assessment, you will be able to discern how the Ancestral Lines Clearing modality works for you and how to use it again for other family traits.

Chapter Ten

Ancestral Lines Clearing Scripts

Preparation for clearing each side of your family

1. Select the issue you want to use for your Ancestral Lines Clearing.

2. Enter into trance state and attune yourself to the will of your High Self.

3. Ask your High Self:

a. What facet of this issue is the most effective yet easiest to clear at this time?

b. Which side of your family seems to be the most strongly connected to the facet?

c. What spiritual element will be used at its highest-power to clear your ancestral lines of this facet?

d. What is the symbol of this side of your ancestral lines?

e. How are you to use the symbol to follow the clearing, so that you know when the energy stops temporarily and when it is finished with the clearing?

Ho'oponopono Rite and Ancestral Lines Clearing

1. Ho'oponopono Rite is done in group format, not individually.

a. Call in your High Self, ask that it surround you and fill you with its highest, purest spiritual light.

b. Picture all members of this side of your family at a comfortable distance in front of you. Let them be surrounded and filled with the light of their choosing. Do nothing to their light.

c. As sincerely as possible, forgive them *as a group,* for the facet of the issue chosen. Pause and let it sink in. Then accept their forgiveness of you for the same facet. Pause and let it sink in.

d. Let family members disappear from the group as they will.

e. If anyone still stays in the picture, do the forgiveness rite with them again in group format. Then finally individually.

2. After all family members have left the scene, ask your High Self to replenish your light.

a. Direct it to clear the same family lines, using the high-powered element chosen.

b. Watch what transpires. Do not try to do any of the clearing work yourself.

c. Any time the energy dies down and you know the clearing is not finished, perform the Ho'oponopono rite to that time period. Do this even if you have no c l u e what had transpired.

d. Ask your High Self resume the clearing, if it does not do so on its own.

e. When your symbol shows that the work is f i n i s h e d, return to the present.

f. Ask your High Self to replenish your energy.

Subsequent Sides of Your Family

Using the same issue as the other side of the family, follow the same instructions as in all segments of Ancestral Lines Clearing above, until all is cleared. Then continue with the following sections.

Clearing Your Future

1. Ask your High Self:

a. What spiritual element will be used at its highest power to clear your future of this facet?

b. What is the symbol of your future?

c. How are you to use the symbol to follow the clearing, so that you know when the energy stops temporarily and when it is finished with the clearing?

2. Direct your High Self to clear your own life's future up through and beyond your death.

    a. Say the Ho'oponopono rite only if there is a block somewhere in the future.

    b. When your future is cleared, ask your High Self to replenish your energy.

"Doorstep"

Ask your High Self to take the healing up to the doorstep of every living family member, whether known or unknown. Trust that it will not bring it to the doorstep of anyone who would abuse the gift. All others will take it or leave it according to their own spiritual guidance.

Personal Follow-ups Scripts

Remember, "soul part removal" needs to be done prior to changing beliefs. This is to safe-guard accuracy of beliefs-change. Someone else's soul parts on you could deceive you into thinking a belief is yours when it really is not.

1. Soul Part Removal

    a. Ask your High Self to identify and send others' soul parts to their respective High Selves. Do not send them directly to the person to whom they belong; to do so is to do an unasked-for healing, which is against divinely given free will.

    b. Fill your vacated spaces with your energy and that of the High Self.

    c. Experience the change.

2. Beliefs Change

    a. Beliefs Removal. Ask your High Self to locate a dysfunctional belief directly relating to the issue-facet you just cleared. Discuss it as needed.

        1). Ask your High Self to take the power out of the belief.

        2). Experience the change.

    b. Do not stop there, or the void will only pull the dysfunctional belief back to you.

    c. Beliefs Replacement. Ask your High Self for the exact wording of the replacement belief. Discuss and revise it as needed.

1). Ask your High Self to put power into that new belief.

2). Experience the change.

Anchoring the Healing

1. Ask your High Self to spread its powerful light clear through you. Rest in that energy.

2. Ask your High Self to take all healing and beneficial changes of this session deep into every molecule of your being, physical and non-physical, known and unknown, to help you adapt to the beneficial changes.

3. Be receptive; let the High Self's energy anchor the healing within you.

4. Experience the change.

5. Retrace your steps and return out of the journey.

Chapter Eleven

My Shamanic Path

Signs of the Path

In tribal cultures throughout the world, shamans are chosen by Spirit rather than by the genetic heritage way that our western countries have chosen royalty. The spiritual choice manifests in the budding shaman in any of various ways, such as Near-Death Experiences, psychic ability, prophecy, mediumship, gifts of spiritual healing, visions, ability to communicate with animals, spiritual initiations, "Big Dreams," to name a few. The individual who reports any one of these experiences is immediately taken under the wing of the shaman, to be trained further. Often, the shaman is called "the wounded healer." This means that she/he finds ways to heal self, and through doing so, discovers powerful ways to heal others.

Our western culture lost its shamanic path centuries ago. As a result, many children who now report such abilities have been shamed and discounted, rather than helped to develop in a healthy and ethical way. Seemingly, those who are lucky enough to have family members who are interested in metaphysics or have experienced psychic phenomena themselves, have allowed their abilities to survive.

In that respect I was lucky. Both sides of my family have a long history of creativity of all kinds. My mother and her mother had repeated spontaneous psychic experiences. Mom embraced and encouraged any such abilities I had and gently guided me to TV programs and printed articles on the subject. She was not interested in metaphysics, per se, so she had no way of guiding me to anyone who could help me develop accordingly. But at least she did not discount me for having them.

Shamanic Signposts

If I had grown up in a tribal culture, any one of the following that I have experienced would have been a sufficient sign for the shaman to set me onto the shamanic path.

Channeling. I am a life long musician. During performances I often feel like I am channeling Spirit through the music, working in tandem with the vibration and musical expression of the people present. As a choral conductor I felt I was working with invisible energies, which resulted in a more inspiring musical expression from the singers. I attribute this ability to work with and conduct energies as my preparation for doing shamanic work such as soul retrievals, shamanic healing and calling on angelic help during depossession and aura cleansing work. My modality-specific channeled material includes Soul Transformation© and Ancestral Lines Clearing©.

Spontaneous Visions. At about age three I clairvoyantly saw a shining, white-robed man who gave me a message of encouragement.

Mediumship Ability. For a few weeks in 1979 after my mother and brother Jim died in a house fire, they communicated with me in numerous "visits" which I experienced clairvoyantly. Since that time, when someone I know dies, I can mentally call out, "I am here if you need to talk." Sometimes they come by and sometimes they do not.

"Big" Dreams. "Big" dreams are vivid ones that often carry a strongly spiritual message. Within a few days after their deaths, my brothers Steve and Rob showed up in my dreams to say goodbye. Years later, Rob came to me in a dream to help me finish an oil painting I was doing of him.

Some of my "Big" dreams are precognitive in a way that are not fully recognized until after the events begin manifesting. However, ever since November of 1978, every time I dream about Christmas, someone I know dies. (At least three of the dreams were documented ahead of the fateful events.) All but two did not contain the person's identity, so I could not warn them. Spirit said this was because the person's spirit intended them to leave; warning them would not have changed that. The dream was meant only to keep me from being devastated by the loss.

On January 8, 1979, I dreamt of my parents' house-fire (I was in South Carolina and they lived in Pennsylvania) at the exact time it happened. I saw the position of my mother as she succumbed, and I felt the awesome euphoria she experienced as she left her body. Two days later, the fire men found both Mom and Jim at the exact spots and wearing the very clothing I had seen in the dream. In the first part of the dream, my witnessing position was a half-story higher than that house's construction; it was as if I were suspended in midair. A year later, my father rebuilt on top of the old foundation; the current house is a half-story higher than the old house!

Initiation Dreams in 1979. During a research project with the Association for Research and Enlightenment (A.R.E.), founded by Edgar Cayce in Virginia Beach, Virginia, I had a significant dream of the Christ. His deep blue eyes evoked a vibration in me that resonated through every molecule of my body, continuing for a half hour after I woke up.

Throughout that fall my dreams contained many geometrical forms and involved studies within "universities." I was not enrolled in college, and such themes were not the norm for my dreams. Research since then indicates that these themes are common prior to the onset of a major spiritual initiation. During the same time period I also began to have benign precognitive dreams for the first time in my life.

Psychic Abilities. Also during the fall of 1979, my psychic abilities increased dramatically: telepathy, remote viewing, clairvoyance, and clairaudience. It was very puzzling, because I was not actively trying to develop them. These abilities have progressively strengthened through the years of daily meditation, other forms of inner access and now dramatically so with shamanic work.

Spiritual Initiation. On December 9, 1979, I experienced a major spiritual initiation that started at church. Clairvoyantly and clairaudiently I became aware of a group of saints or holy ones in Spirit (not physically present), robed in white, standing before me. One of them put a scepter to the crown of my head while the rest intoned a holy chant. I felt a strong, yet subtle, emanation or vibration that descended into me, pervading my whole body and lasting for nearly seven hours. No one else could see my body vibrating; only I could feel it. One of these holy beings told me of the tests I would be given and the emotional hardships I would go through over the subsequent ten years. He also told me of the beauties of Spirit that would result from it. Then I noticed a deep royal blue color pervading everything I saw, yet it did not change nor distort other colors in any way. This color lasted for six hours.

<u>Intense Interest In Metaphysical Subjects</u>. After that initiation, my interest in metaphysics increased and I took nearly every class that came my way. Like a starving person at a smorgasbord, I could not get enough!

Reluctant Shaman

For fifteen years the shamanic path pulled at me incessantly. It simultaneously fascinated and repulsed me, intrigued and bored me. I sensed a profound depth to it but could not discern any details of how to access the heart of it. I tried to study it from books and through workshops with elders of various Native American tribes, but I always came away with a sense of two-dimensions in a three-dimensional metaphysical world.

I also had mistaken beliefs about shamanism, mistaken because of my incomplete knowledge of what it was all about. I saw individual tribes in their traditional costumes doing their tribal ceremonies. None fit into my modern day world. I could not see myself standing in a public high school classroom wearing tribal clothing and performing tribal music.

I heard whispers about communication with spirits and interpreted that as talking with the dead. This frightened me no end, partly because of a scary incident at age five of seeing an ugly ghost hanging onto my alcoholic great-uncle. This was also frightening due to my untrained mediumship ability and the awareness of how easy the astral realm can deceive.

I heard about worship of the Ancestors and thought, "A dead grandfather is no wiser than a live one. No way can I worship another human. God, only!" At the time, I did not realize that "spirits" is another way of saying "angels," and

"Ancestor" may include a "Spirit Teacher" in addition to family ancestors.

All the while resisting the shamanic path's beckoning, I delved more deeply into metaphysics. Every class, workshop, retreat and study group on any subject available, you name it, I have probably studied it! My study culminated in ordination at Sancta Sophia Seminary in Tahlequah, Oklahoma. This interfaith, metaphysical seminary was founded by Carol Parrish, who is part Cherokee.

My life got ever more turbulent as I continued to resist the shamanic path. Spiritual law says that if we do not obey the call of our soul, the "Lords of Karma" (tests brought by Spirit that feel difficult to withstand) will intensify our lives. Did they ever! A long career teaching high school choral music grew increasingly unsatisfying. I knew I needed to step fully onto the spiritual path, yet fear of the unknown held me back.

Surrendering To The Path

Then one day I had an extremely clear and profound experience: instead of being frightened by the presence of a recently deceased person, I confidently commanded one to go to the Light – successfully, despite not having had instruction on how to do this! That made me realize that I must set foot onto the shamanic path no matter what happened. The moment I committed to that path, doors and avenues miraculously opened for me both during the training period and even later when I set up my shamanic counseling and healing practice. Previously, my inner spiritual guidance was "catch as catch can" erratic. Since stepping on the path, it finally became resoundingly clearer and more accurate. Over the years, I have felt more at one within myself and with all of creation. My faith in Spirit has multiplied exponentially and this trust has not been betrayed.

The moment I surrendered to the shamanic path, I sought out a professor in graduate school who is a shamanic practitioner and asked him to help me begin the process. My first step was to take the Basic Core Shamanism workshop with anthropologist Michael Harner. The shamanic journeying he taught was "old home week" in familiarity, uncannily similar to the Jewish mystical Kabbalah meditations.

Core Shamanism ethics, like tribal ethics, includes a reverence for the Earth and a respect for all kingdoms in nature. That reverence has been part of me since birth. There is also a deep grounding, a practicality, about all aspects of core shamanism: grounding in the Earth, in specific safeguards, in respect for spirit helpers, in seriousness of purpose, and in insistence on playing out into life the wisdom gained during journeying. I have worked with and towards this all my life. Even in my music career, I felt a need to take what I heard within and convey it outwardly through performance and teaching. Just thinking about doing something is insufficient. It needs to be applied in life.

I have been a wounded healer. That means that I came into my current healing profession by first seeking healing for myself. This life is a karmic one, in which I am clearing up the loose ends of all my other lives on the planet. It requires looking into past causes for current problems. It also has required looking for this life's purpose both for self-healing and for helping others. During all of this retro-focus, Spirit has given me insights and ways to access depths of the human spirit seldom found elsewhere. Spirit also gave me the gift to see, in trance, where others' difficulties are coming from and to help them attain the healing they request.

This life has been blessed with coincidences and serendipity in many ways. Clearly, Spirit has been working "behind the scenes." I marvel at how I "just happened onto" the exactly right teachers, musically and spiritually. They were ones with strong integrity who gave well-grounded, practical instruction. The same is true of organizations with whom I became acquainted throughout my spiritual search, and friends who brought to town the right metaphysically–oriented therapists I needed for further healing. Clearly, Spirit and my spirit helpers have been guiding me along the straight and narrow path of transformation. As my shamanic work developed, guidance previously hidden has now emerged into full sight, albeit clairvoyantly within me. Archangels Michael and Raphael, as well as others, came forward in a shamanic journey to tell me they would be working with me in my healing work. Years later when I learned Aura Cleansing, that team escalated their aid to the point that now they incorporate nearly every modality I offer, shamanic or non-shamanic, in my healing work with clients.

During my career as a high school choral music teacher, I often thanked Spirit for allowing me to make a living doing something I loved that often uplifted me in the midst of it. I also knew that teaching was not the end mission for my life. Rather, it was an all around support while I did my in-depth healing of karmic issues, in preparation for this current mission.

In preparation for this healing mission, I gravitated towards schools that required experiential, altered-state work as a partner to intellectual learning: Sancta Sophia Seminary, The Naropa Institute, and the Alchemy Institute of Denver. As a life long musician, I see it as common sense that a person would not take music lessons from someone who had never learned how to play the instrument. Why, then, go to a counselor who had not experienced therapy?! We best know where someone else is coming from if we first experience it ourselves.

In both music and shamanic counseling there is a two-sided rose: as we help others, we better understand our own abilities and selves. As we improve our own abilities and selves, we more fully understand how to help others.

My Educational Background
Music Education
- B.A., Gettysburg College, Pennsylvania
- M.Ed.,The Pennsylvania State University
- 31 years' teaching high school award-winning choral music

Metaphysical Education
- Ordained Minister from the Light of Christ Community Church, Tahlequah, OK
- Integrated Awareness training with Connie Newton

Counseling Education
- Pastoral Counselor Certification, Sancta Sophia Seminary (LCCC), Tahlequah, OK
- Transpersonal Counseling Psychology, 42 M.A. Credits, The Naropa Institute, CO
- Certified Master Hypnotherapist: Alchemy Institute of CO and The American Council of Hypnotist Examiners
- Past-Life Regression Therapist certified by Dolores Cannon
- Certified Thought Field Therapist

<u>Shamanism Training</u>
- Core Shamanism training with Michael Harner, and faculty of the Foundation for Shamanic Studies
- Soul Retrieval and Death & Dying trainings with Sandra Ingerman
- Celtic Shamanism study with Tom Cowan
- Munay Ki Initiations from Vickie Penninger

<u>Spiritual Energy Training</u>
- Depossession study: Hypnotherapy ala Irene Hickman, Shamanic with Betsy Bergstrom, Intuitive as Aura Cleansing with Julia Hanline and Diana Henderson
- Reconnection® training: Dr. Eric Pearl
- Karmic Matrix Clearing certification, Rev. Jeannie Montague
- Reiki Master
- Black Hat Feng Shui with Rev. Sue Ruzicka and others

Teachings From My Spirit Guides

As extensive as my human-taught educational background is, the vast majority of my training and teaching since June of 1994 has come from my spirit guides, i.e., power animals, spirit teachers, angels and archangels.

The following are three significant modalities that have proved powerfully healing in many people's lives. They were channeled to me by my primary spirit teachers. Initial copyright and published copyright dates are shown.
- Ancestral Lines Clearing: © 1996, 2000, 2012
- Soul Transformation after a soul retrieval: © 1996, 2010
- Clearing Ancestral Karmic Lines: © 1998, 2000

Some of the work that I learned from other humans has been transformed, added to or modified by my spirit guides to fit a shamanic framework. These include:
- Feng Shui
- Past-Life Regression within the shamanic journey
- Karmic Matrix Clearing
- Soul Retrieval
- Various shamanic healing methods

Glossary

This Glossary's terminology is arranged primarily by category in order to give you a more cohesive understanding of the general framework of Ancestral Lines Clearing.

Metaphysical Terms

Channeling. This is a process of Spirit using the human to convey its messages of guidance, healing, and inspiration to other humans. It can be done by a specific Spirit directly using the person's voice to persons present to the channeler, or by conveying the message to the channeler telepathically and the channeler conveys that to her/his audience.

Chakras is a Hindu term for the energy vortices in our bodies. There are seven major ones along the spine to the top of the head: base of the spine, mid-belly, solar plexus, heart, throat, middle of the forehead ("third eye"), and the crown. There are also at least two healing chakras in the palms of the hands, and numerous other more minor ones throughout the limbs.

Clairaudience, Clairsentience and Clairvoyance are French words adopted by psychic people to describe what the mind can perceive psychically without the use of the physical senses. Clairaudience is hearing sounds or words in the mind. Clairsentience is sensing or feeling information that is not conveyed through physical sensing. Clairvoyance is seeing images in the mind without the use of the physical eyes.

The Dark is a commonly used term in metaphysical circles to denote evil. It has nothing to do with color. Rather, it relates to that which is difficult to see, because it fades into the background in order to hide unethical or immoral acts.

Dharma is a Hindu term used to define destiny and gifts from past-lives.

Karma, aka karmic debt, is a Hindu term used to define difficulties coming from past-life errors. It is a "hands-on" learning process in life. As long as you fall back into the "old" way of thinking, feeling and acting, you will continue to have instances in your life that bring up the pain and hardship that is part of your karma. A spiritual goal of life is to learn how to think, feel and act in a new way, i.e., not be constrained by that specific issue. It is only then that those old experiences either will bring up a totally new attitude or emotion in you, or you will be mysteriously "whisked" away from circumstances that would bring them up once again.

"The Light" is a commonly used term in metaphysics: (1) for that spiritual realm that some religions call heaven; (2) for the spiritual forces of good; (3) spiritual energy of the good that is used for various forms of healing and for transmuting the dark.

Psychological Terms

"Block" is a common term indicating inability to move forward in your healing or spiritual growth, no matter how hard you try. It is an indication of something hidden within your mind and psychology that prohibits positive change.

"Issue" is a term that indicates a dysfunctional facet of your personality. It will cause negative emotions such as anger, irritation, fear, doubt, to name a few, to arise within you. It will cause projection. When it is healed or removed, you will feel relief or peace. What caused it will no longer be a negative force (issue) within you.

"Projection" occurs when you deny a fault within yourself. Your subconscious then brings it to your awareness by revving up your emotions and pointing your attention onto someone else. You see in that person what you secretly deem to be your own worst fault. (Verb form: pro'ject, with the accent on the second syllable.)

Shamanic Terms

Core Shamanism: the core of what all shamanic cultures worldwide do for their people. However, there is no specific religion nor style of ceremonies connected to core shamanism. Practitioners bring to it their own religions and practices.

High Self. This is a Hawaiian shamanism term that equates to a personal Mother-Father God who watches over you and is the guiding force for you and your spirit guides. Some also call it the "I-Am Presence." See the "Huna" chapter for details.

Shamanism: the spiritual practice ascribed to tribal cultures worldwide that we often think of as based in the psychic and holistic: readings, spiritual healing, prophecy, communicating with animals and plants telepathically, soul retrieval, carrying the deceased's spirit to the Light, finding where there is food, finding past causes of current problems, and more. Each tribe has a specific set of spiritual beliefs and ceremonial practices interwoven with what the shaman does for the tribe. Outwardly, tribes around the world differ widely from each other, yet all shamans get similar results with their people.

Shaman: someone who has the effective ability to work with Spirit in many of the healing ways indicated in the previous paragraph. In tribal cultures, the shaman also is a member of the tribe. In today's age, many countries have lost their tribal connections, yet all humans are descendants of some time-distant tribal culture.

Shamanic Practitioner: another term for a human who practices various aspects of core shamanism, such as those delineated under "shamanism" above.

Shamanic Realms of the Upper, Middle and Lower Worlds: the three parallel dimensions used in shamanism. The middle world is where we live in physical body and in our minds. The upper world inwardly looks like sky and clouds and is where the spirit teacher lives. The lower world inwardly looks like our pristine wilderness and is where the power animal lives. (Note: the lower world is not "hell." Shamans say if there is a "hell" it is in the middle world.) Non-Ordinary Reality is that part of the middle world where we think, pray, create, meditate, go into trance. The upper and lower worlds also are part of non-ordinary reality. Ordinary Reality is the physical form of middle world.

Shamanic Journey: a self-induced trance using a fast monotonous rhythm to take the mind into deeper levels. The most commonly used rhythmical sounds are drums and rattles. This is done to obtain guidance and healing from your own spirit guides, who are mostly of the angelic evolution.

In this form of trance, there is inner imagery of traveling into one of three parallel dimensions connected to the Earth: the non-ordinary reality of the upper, middle and lower worlds. While the non-ordinary realms make use of imagination, that does not mean it is false. Quite the contrary. The imagination is where all creative endeavors originate. Imagery may feel like day dreaming or in some way forced, if it originates from the mind. It flows when it originates from Spirit. The truth in journey information often appears suddenly or unexpectedly, appearing without any effort on your part. Often there is also a pervasive and deep sense of "this is the truth!"

Soul Parts: pieces of a person's soul that have split off from you into what is called "soul loss." It does this for any of myriad different reasons. Soul Loss. If a soul part splits off from the physical, emotional and mental part of you, it goes into what shamans call "soul loss." It stays connected to you at the spiritual level, but not at the other levels. It cannot return on its own and it has no emotional nor mental contact with you. It continues to carry the spiritual traits with which it is supposed to help you, but you have no access to that until it is retrieved for you.

Spiritual Terms

Kingdom of Angels: This is a different although parallel evolutionary path to that of the Human Kingdom. They have been with us in all world cultures and religions since the beginning of human life on this planet, perhaps even before. They are here to guard and guide us. Each of our angels is linked to and under the jurisdiction of our High Self, i.e., God who watches over us and answers prayer.

The angelic kingdom is invisible to the naked eye because of being in a dimension that vibrates so fast that it cannot be experienced through our physical senses. It is discerned with our inner imagery senses otherwise known as clairvoyance, clairaudience, clairsentience. Angels' true form is Light. They show up clairvoyantly as angels with wings, human, animal, sense of presence or pure light, according to what will best help us. Archangels, including Michael and Raphael, are part of this kingdom.

Power Animals: This is actually a shamanic term for the spirit guides who appear as animals, to the mind's eye. They are highly intelligent and spiritual and also are predominantly of the Angelic Kingdom. They appear in animal form to give us an instant recognition of the traits with which they will help us.

Soul. This is your unique self or essence, given to you by Highest Spirit. No one else's soul can substitute for it. The soul has a spirit but is not the same as spirit. The Greeks call the soul "psyche" and the spirit "pneuma."

Spirit. This is my "catch-all" term for God, Creator, Allah, Universe, angels, spirit guides or any other term you may choose to delineate highest Spirit and all invisible beings that work for the highest good.

Spirit Guides: spiritual beings, usually of the angelic evolution, who are assigned by Highest Spirit to guide and guard us. A few deceased humans may be assigned by Highest Spirit to serve as spirit guides, but this is not the norm.

Spirit Helpers: a "catch-all" term for spirit guides, spirit teachers, power animals, angels.

Spirit Teacher: the shamanic term corresponding to a spirit guide who usually appears in human form, to the mind's eye.

Bibliography

Huna
Enid Hoffman. Huna, A Beginner's Guide. Whitford Press, division of Schiffer Publishing, Ltd. ISBN 0-914918-03-6

Max Freedom Long. The Secret Science At Work. DeVorss & Co., Pub. ISBN 0-87516-046-8

Max Freedom Long. The Secret Science Behind Miracles. DeVorss & Co., Pub. ISBN 0-87516-047-6

Max Freedom Long. The Huna Code In Religions. DeVorss & Co., Pub. ISBN 0-87516-495-1

Arlyn J. Macdonald. Essential Huna. Barnes & Noble or InfinityPublishing.com/ ISBN 0-7414-1373-6

Erika Nau. Self Awareness Through Huna. The Donning Company/Publishers. ISBN 0-89865-099-2

Shamanism
Tom Cowan, PhD. Shamanism as a Spiritual Practice for Daily Life. The Crossing Press, Freedom, CA. ISBN 0-89594-838-9

Michael Harner. The Way of the Shaman. Bantam Books, Harper & Row, Pub. ISBN 0-553-25982-2

Sandra Ingerman. Soul Retrieval, Mending the Fragmented Self. HarperSanFrancisco. ISBN 0-06-250406-1

Sandra Ingerman. Shamanic Journeying, a Beginner's Guide. Sounds True, Boulder, CO. ISBN 1-59179-151-0

Resources

Core Shamanism

Michael Harner is an American anthropologist who first introduced the practice of core shamanism to our modern society.

Sandra Ingerman, former educational director for the Foundation for Shamanic Studies (FSS), was the first to bring soul retrieval to the world's awareness.

The Foundation for Shamanic Studies (FSS) was founded by Michael Harner. Its intentions are to provide outreach to still existing shamanic cultures, and to keep the core shamanism practices pure. This is so that anyone can learn them if they wish to, regardless of culture. Its website is www.shamanism.org/

The Society of Shamanic Practitioners (SSP) was founded by Sandra Ingerman, Tom Cowan and other members of FSS. Its intention is to provide avenues for shamanic journeyers to receive more advanced instruction and report on shamanic research beyond what FSS gives. FSS and SSP are excellent adjuncts for each other. www.shamansociety.org/

Metaphysical

Aura Cleansing was independently channelled by Julia Hanline and Diana Henderson. Upon comparing what Archangel Michael taught them about energy cleansing and transmuting discarnate spirits, they found that the information was virtually the same, aside from a few small personal details. The work is effective and swift in application. Julia's website is: www.thespiritualmentor.wordpress.com/ Diana's website is: www.OrderofMichael.com/

The Light of Christ Community Church and Sancta Sophia Seminary were founded by Rev. Carol Parrish in Tahlequah, OK. The seminary teaches profound truths within metaphysical lore as well as many faiths throughout the world and history. It teaches those who wish to grow spiritually, ordains ministers, and confers degrees for advanced studies. www.sanctasophia.org/

52715031R00062

Made in the USA
Middletown, DE
21 November 2017